MW01277992

Copyright © Rosemary King, 2020

All rights Reserved. No part of this publication or the information in it may be quoted from or reproduced in any form by means such as printing, scanning, photocopying or otherwise without prior written permission of the copyright holder.

Disclaimer and Terms of Use: Effort has been made to ensure that the information in this book is accurate and complete, however, the author and the publisher do not warrant the accuracy of the information, text and graphics contained within the book due to the rapidly changing nature of science, research, known and unknown facts and internet. The Author and the publisher do not hold any responsibility for errors, omissions or contrary interpretation of the subject matter herein. This book is presented solely for motivational and informational purposes only.

CONTENTS

3

4

INTRODUCTION

Air fryer is a brand new kitchen appliance that can cook almost all types of food in an easier and healthier way. The process of cooking in the air fryer helps to reduce the using of oil and fats to 25 % - 30 %. It is a real super machine in comparison with other ways of cooking. The circulating hot air around the food helps to cook the meal with crispy effect. If previously, the Maillard effect was possible to get only by boiling in oil or fat – now you can cook the meal just with the small amount of it. The air fryer makes the process of cooking very suitable for people who get used to eating healthy food. Just imagine that you can cook your favorite potato chips, chicken nuggets or fish fries without any doubts about their usefulness.

The air fryer can have an adjustable temperature mode that will help you to cook the meal fast and get the desired effect. The air fryer that does not have temperature mode is also possible to use but it should have strict temperature chart. As usual, every machine has the manufacturer directions that can make the cooking process easier.

There is the wrong statement that food can be coked by itself – you should shake the ingredients during the cooking. Of course, there are some exceptions to the recipe.
Some air fryers have the food agitator – so you will not need to think about stirring the meal.

The air fryers have different sizes that can be appropriate for the various amount of people. You can choose the air fryer for a big family or that one which will be good only for two. The most recommended size of the air fryer for 2 people is 1.8 lb.

The air fryer cannot substitute you all the kitchen appliances but it can save your time and cook tasty food!

BREAKFAST

BROCCOLI PARMESAN CASSEROLE

Prep time: 10 min | Cooking time: 12 min | Servings: 2

INGREDIENTS:

6 oz chicken, cooked	3 oz Parmesan, shredded
5 oz broccoli, boiled	1 tbsp panko breadcrumbs
2 tsp mayonnaise	1 tsp garlic powder
1 pinch salt	½ tsp butter
¼ cup cream	

DIRECTIONS:

Preheat the air fryer to 360 F. Chop the chicken and broccoli into the medium cubes. Then combine mayonnaise and cream together. Sprinkle the mixture with the salt, garlic powder, and butter. Whisk it. Place the chopped chicken in the glass form. Then cover the chicken with the ½ part of all mayonnaise mixture. Make the layer of the chopped broccoli and spread it with the remaining mayonnaise mixture. Cover the casserole with the panko breadcrumbs. Put the casserole in the air fryer and cook for 12 min. When the casserole is cooked – serve it.

NUTRITION:

calories 354, fat 16.4, fiber 2.1, carbs 11.8, protein 41.3

CHICKEN SAUSAGES

Prep time: 10 min | Cooking time: 15 min | Servings: 2

INGREDIENTS:

7 oz ground chicken	1 egg
½ tsp chili flakes	½ tsp onion powder
1 tsp butter	½ tsp garlic powder

1 pinch salt — black pepper
1 pinch ground — ½ tsp canola oil

DIRECTIONS:

Put the ground chicken in the bowl. Sprinkle the ground chicken with the chili flakes, butter, onion powder, garlic powder, salt, and ground black pepper. Beat the egg in the ground chicken. Then mix it up with the help of the fingertips. When the forcemeat is cooked – make the sausages. Sprinkle the sausages with the canola oil. Put the air fryer to 360 F. Cook the sausages for 15 min. Turn the sausages into another part after 10 min of cooking. Serve the sausages hot.

NUTRITION:

calories 252, fat 12.6, fiber 0.1, carbs 1.2, protein 31.7

OATS CARROT COOKIES

Prep time: 10 min | Cooking time: 8 min | Servings: 2

INGREDIENTS:

1 carrot	cinnamon
3 tbsp oatmeal	¼ tsp baking soda
1 egg	
1 tbsp butter	1 tbsp sour cream
2 tsp sugar	
¼ tsp ground	

DIRECTIONS:

Peel the carrot and grate it. Put the grated carrot in the bowl. Beat the egg in the grated carrot. Sprinkle the mixture with the oatmeal, butter, sugar, ground cinnamon, baking soda, and sour cream. Mix it up with the help of the spoon. Then make 2 big balls from the carrot mixture. Flatten them gently. Preheat the air fryer to 360 F. Put the carrot cookies in the air fryer rack and cook them for 10 min. When the cookies are cooked – they will be still soft. Serve them warm.

calories 153, fat 9.7, fiber 1.7, carbs 12.9, protein 4.3

AVOCADO CHEDDAR ROLLS
Prep time: 10 min | Cooking time: 10 min | Servings: 2

INGREDIENTS:

½ avocado, pitted	4 bacon slices
2 slices Cheddar cheese	¼ tsp paprika
	1 tsp olive oil

DIRECTIONS:
Peel the avocado and mash it with the help of the fork. Add paprika and stir the mixture carefully. After this, put 2 bacon slices beside each other and spread them with the mashed avocado. Add 1 slice of Cheddar cheese and roll it. Make the same steps with the remaining bacon. Secure the rolls with the toothpicks. The bacon should cover all the cheese. After this, preheat the air fryer to 360 F. Place avocado roll in the air fryer. Cook the meal for 10 min. Stir it once during the cooking. When the rolls are cooked – serve them immediately.

NUTRITION:
calories 442, fat 37.3, fiber 3.5, carbs 5.4, protein 22

TURMERIC POTATO PANCAKES
Prep time: 10 min | Cooking time: 4 min | Servings: 2

INGREDIENTS:

6 oz mashed potato	¼ tsp ground thyme
1 tbsp flour	2 oz white onion, diced
1 pinch salt	1 tsp canola oil
1 egg	
1 tsp turmeric	

DIRECTIONS:
Put the mashed potato in the bowl and crack the egg there. Add salt and flour. After this, sprinkle the mashed potato with the turmeric, ground thyme, and diced white onion. Mix the mixture with the help of the hand mixer. Then make the balls from the mashed potato mixture and flatten them with the help of the palms to get the pancake shape. Preheat the air fryer to 365 F. Sprinkle the air fryer basket with the canola oil inside. Put the pancakes there and cook them for 4 min from each side. When the pancakes are cooked – they will have the light brown color of the surface. Enjoy the pancakes hot. Sprinkle the pancakes with the sour cream if desired.

NUTRITION:
calories 178, fat 8.3, fiber 2.3, carbs 21, protein 5.3

CHEDDAR EGGS BURRITO
Prep time: 10 min | Cooking time: 8 min | Servings: 2

INGREDIENTS:

2 eggs	1 tbsp mayonnaise
½ avocado, pitted	1 pinch salt
½ sweet red pepper	1 pinch ground black pepper
2 slices Cheddar cheese	1 corn tortilla

DIRECTIONS:
Beat the eggs in the bowl and whisk them. Sprinkle the whisked eggs with the salt and ground black pepper. Pour the whisked egg mixture into the air fryer tray. Preheat the air fryer to 365 F and put the whisked egg there. Cook the eggs for 5 min. After this, remove the cooked eggs from the air fryer. Spread

the corn tortilla with the mayonnaise. Put the cooked eggs over the mayonnaise layer. Then cut the sweet red pepper into the strips and put them on the corn tortilla too. Add Cheddar cheese slices. Slice the avocado and add it to the corn tortilla too. After this, roll the corn tortilla to get the burrito. Preheat the air fryer to 365 F. Put the burrito there and cook it for 3 min. When the burrito is cooked – remove it from the air fryer and cut into 2 parts.

NUTRITION:
calories 343, fat 26.3, fiber 4.5, carbs 14.4, protein 14.5

SCRAMBLED EGGS
Prep time: 10 min | Cooking time: 17 min | Servings: 2

INGREDIENTS:

1 tsp butter	thyme
4 eggs	1 pinch salt
¼ tsp ground	1 tsp paprika

DIRECTIONS:
Preheat the air fryer to 345 F. Toss the butter in the air fryer basket and melt it for 3 min. Meanwhile, crack the eggs and whisk them. Sprinkle the whisked eggs with the ground thyme, salt, and paprika. Stir the egg mixture gently. After this, pour the egg mixture into the air fryer basket. Cook the eggs for 5 min at 345 F. Then scramble the egg carefully and cook them for 5 min more at the same temperature. After this, scramble the eggs one more time and cook at 365 F for 4 min more. Transfer the cooked scrambled eggs in the serving plates.

NUTRITION:
calories 146, fat 10.8, fiber 0.4, carbs 1.4, protein 11.3

TURKEY BREAD REUBEN
Prep time: 10 min | Cooking time: 10 min | Servings: 2

INGREDIENTS:

5 oz turkey fillet, roasted	1 tbsp mayonnaise
4 slices grey bread	1 tsp pesto
3 oz Swiss cheese	1 tsp tomato sauce

DIRECTIONS:
Slice the roasted turkey. Slice Swiss cheese. After this, combine the mayonnaise, pesto, and tomato sauce in the shallow bowl. Stir it. Spread the bread slices with the mayonnaise mixture. Then put the turkey slices and cheese slices onto 2 bread slices. Cover them with the 2 remaining grey bread slices. Preheat the air fryer to 320 F. Put the Reuben in the air fryer and cook for 10 min. When the turkey Reuben cooked – serve the meal immediately.

NUTRITION:
calories 370, fat 19.5, fiber 0.5, carbs 13.5, protein 33.9

ENGLISH EGGS BACON BREAKFAST
Prep time: 10 min | Cooking time: 16 min | Servings: 2

INGREDIENTS:

2 slices bacon	paprika
2 sausages	2 eggs
¼ tsp salt	2 bread slices
¼ tsp ground	¼ tsp olive oil

DIRECTIONS:
Preheat the air fryer to 355 F. Place the bacon slices and sausages on the back rack. Cook the ingredients for 6 min. After this, turn the bacon slices and sausages onto another side and cook for 7 min more. Then transfer

the cooked bacon and sausages on the serving plates. After this, sprinkle the ramekins with the olive oil and beat the eggs there. Cook the eggs for 3 min at 300 F. Place the ramekins with eggs on the plate with the cooked sausages and bacon. Add the bread slices.

NUTRITION:
calories 240, fat 16.9, fiber 0.3, carbs 5.3, protein 15.8

TURMERIC POTATO
Prep time: 10 min | Cooking time: 25 min | Servings: 2

INGREDIENTS:

1 tsp ghee	½ tsp salt
2 big potatoes	½ tsp ground
1 sweet yellow	black pepper
pepper	½ tsp onion
1 white onion,	powder
sliced	½ tsp turmeric

DIRECTIONS:
Wash the potatoes carefully and cut them into the medium cubes. Preheat the air fryer to 365 F. Put the potato cubes in the big bowl. Add water and leave the vegetables for 10 min. After this, drain the potatoes and dry with the help of the paper towel. Place the potato cubes in the air fryer and add ghee. Cook the potatoes for 15 min. Then shake the potatoes and cook for 4 min more. Meanwhile, remove the seeds from the sweet yellow pepper and cut it into the strips. Combine the pepper strips with the sliced onion. After this, combine the turmeric, onion powder, ground black pepper, and salt in the shallow bowl. Stir it gently. Put the pepper-onion mixture in the air fryer. Sprinkle the mixture with spices and shake gently. Cook the meal for 6 min at 370 F. Then shake the cooked meal again.

NUTRITION:
calories 326, fat 2.8, fiber 11.2, carbs 70.2, protein 7.9

MILKY VANILLA TOASTS
Prep time: 15 min | Cooking time: 5 min | Servings: 2

INGREDIENTS:

1 egg	2 tbsp milk
4 bread slices	1 tbsp sugar
1 tsp vanilla	2 tsp butter
extract	

DIRECTIONS:
Beat the egg in the bowl and whisk it until smooth. Then mash the butter with the help of the spoon. Add the vanilla extract in the mashed butter. After this, sprinkle the whisked egg with the milk and sugar. Stir it until sugar is dissolved. After this, spread the bread slices with the mashed butter mixture from both sides. Put the bread slices in the egg-milk mixture and let them soak all the egg liquid. Preheat the air fryer to 400 F. Transfer the bread slices to the air fryer rack. Cook the toasts for 2 min from one side. After this, turn the bread slices to another side and cook for 3 min more. Cut the cooked toasts into triangles.

NUTRITION:
calories 149, fat 6.9, fiber 0.4, carbs 16.3, protein 4.7

CREAMY BACON OMELET
Prep time: 10 min | Cooking time: 24 min | Servings: 2

INGREDIENTS:

2 eggs	1 pinch salt
3 tbsp heavy	¼ tsp cayenne
cream	pepper
3 bacon slices	1 tsp butter
¼ tsp oregano	1 oz fresh dill,

chopped

DIRECTIONS:

Crack the eggs into the mixing bowl and whisk them. Then pour the heavy cream and keep whisking the mixture for 30 seconds more. Preheat the air fryer to 360 F. Place the bacon slices on the air fryer rack and cook it for 5 min from each side. When the bacon is cooked – chill it little and chop. Then sprinkle the egg mixture with the oregano, salt, cayenne pepper, and chopped dill. Spread 2 muffin molds with the butter. Pour the egg mixture there. Sprinkle it with the chopped bacon. Preheat the air fryer to 360 F. Cook the omelet for 14 min.

NUTRITION:

calories 349, fat 27.2, fiber 2.1, carbs 9.5, protein 19.5

BAKED CHEDDAR EGGS

Prep time: 10 min | Cooking time: 5 min | Servings: 2

INGREDIENTS:

2 eggs	1 tsp butter,
2 oz ham	unsalted, soft
3 oz Cheddar cheese, shredded	1 pinch salt
	$\frac{1}{4}$ tsp ground chili pepper

DIRECTIONS:

Preheat the air fryer to 360 F. Take 2 ramekins and spread them with the soft butter. Then slice ham and put it into the ramekins. Beat the eggs into 2 ramekins. Sprinkle the eggs with the salt and ground chili pepper. Sprinkle the eggs with the shredded cheese. Place the ramekins in the preheated air fryer and cook for 5 min. If the eggs are not cooked enough – cook it for 1-2 min more. Let the eggs chill for 1-2 min.

NUTRITION:

calories 297, fat 22.8, fiber 0.4, carbs 2, protein 20.9

BACON ZUCCHINI BOATS

Prep time: 10 min | Cooking time: 12 min | Servings: 2

INGREDIENTS:

1 medium zucchini	black pepper
4 bacon slices	$\frac{1}{2}$ tsp ground ginger
1 pinch salt	1 tsp butter
1 pinch ground	

DIRECTIONS:

Cut the zucchini crosswise to get 2 medium boards. Then rub the zucchini board with the salt, ground black pepper, and ground ginger. Melt the butter and brush the zucchini from each side. Wrap the zucchini boards into bacon slices and secure the vegetables with the toothpicks. Preheat the air fryer to 400 F. Place the wrapped zucchini onto the air fryer rack and cook for 12 min. Turn the zucchini into another side after 6 min of cooking. When the time is over – the bacon will be a little bit crunchy. Dry the zucchini boats with the paper towel.

NUTRITION:

calories 240, fat 18, fiber 1.2, carbs 4.2, protein 15.3

BREAKFAST PARMESAN SANDWICH

Prep time: 10 min | Cooking time: 7 min | Servings: 2

INGREDIENTS:

4 slices sandwich bread	1 tbsp butter
1 tbsp pesto sauce	4 slices Parmesan cheese
	2 slices ham

DIRECTIONS:
Spread two slices of the sandwich bread with the butter. After this, spread another two slices of the sandwich bread with the pesto sauce. Place 2 slices of Parmesan cheese and 1 slice of the ham on the sandwich bread slices. Cover them with the second bread slice. Preheat the air fryer to 365 F. Put the sandwiches in the air fryer rack. Cook the sandwiches for 7 min. After this, chill the cooked sandwiches for 3 min.

NUTRITION:
calories 437, fat 12.1, fiber 1.5, carbs 30.9, protein 24.6

CHEDDAR BAKED PAPRIKA TOASTS
Prep time: 10 min | Cooking time: 7 min | Servings: 2

INGREDIENTS:

2 eggs	ic
2 slices, Cheddar cheese	½ tsp olive oil
2 bread slices	1 tbsp butter, salted
1 pinch paprika	2 leaves fresh
1 pinch turmer-	basil

DIRECTIONS:
Sprinkle 2 ramekins with the olive oil and crack the eggs there. Sprinkle the eggs with the paprika and turmeric. Preheat the air fryer to 300 F. Cook the eggs for 4 min. Meanwhile, spread the bread slices with the butter. When the eggs are cooked – place them over the bread layer. Then place Cheddar cheese over the eggs. Cook the toasts for 3 min at 300 F. When the cheese starts to melt – the toast is cooked.

NUTRITION:
calories 152, fat 5.2, fiber 0.5, carbs 5.9, protein 6.4

EGG HAM ROLLS
Prep time: 10 min | Cooking time: 10 min | Servings: 2

INGREDIENTS:

1 egg, boiled	2 oz ham, chopped
4 egg roll wraps	1 tsp butter
1 garlic clove	½ tsp dried oregano
½ white onion, stewed	1 tsp olive oil

DIRECTIONS:
Peel the boiled eggs and chop them. Combine the chopped eggs with the stewed onion and ham. Then peel the garlic clove and mince it. Add the minced garlic in the chopped egg mixture. Add dried oregano. Melt butter and add it to the egg mixture too. Mix the mixture up. Put the egg mixture on the egg roll wraps and roll them. Preheat the air fryer 380 F. Place the egg rolls in the air fryer rack and spray them with the olive oil. Cook the meal for 10 min. When the egg rolls have the golden brown color – they are cooked. Serve them immediately.

NUTRITION:
calories 349, fat 14.2, fiber 3.4, carbs 40.9, protein 14.5

BUTTERY POTATO SCRAMBLE
Prep time: 10 min | Cooking time: 25 min | Servings: 2

INGREDIENTS:

2 medium potatoes	½ tsp olive oil
2 eggs	1 tsp fresh dill
1 tsp butter	1 tsp fresh parsley
¼ tsp salt	1 tbsp soy sauce
¼ tsp cayenne pepper	

DIRECTIONS:

Peel the potatoes and cut them into the small cubes. Sprinkle the potato cubes with the salt, soy sauce, and cayenne pepper. Shake them well. Preheat the air fryer to 400 F. Toss the butter in the air fryer and cook for 12 min. Meanwhile, crack the eggs into the bowl and whisk them. Combine the whisked eggs with the fresh dill and fresh parsley. Stir it. When the time is over – shake the potatoes well and sprinkle with the olive oil. Then pour the whisked egg mixture over the potatoes and cook the meal for 3 min at 400 F. After this, scramble the potatoes and cook for 10 min more at 360 F. When the meal is cooked – shake it well one more time.

NUTRITION:

calories 243, fat 7.7, fiber 5.3, carbs 34.9, protein 9.8

SUGARY OATMEAL MUFFINS

Prep time: 10 min | Cooking time: 10 min | Servings: 2

INGREDIENTS:

¼ cup butter	1 pinch salt
¼ cup powdered sugar	2 tbsp oatmeal
2 eggs	1 tsp vanilla extract
1 tbsp flour	

DIRECTIONS:

Melt the butter gently and combine it with the powdered sugar. Start to mix the mixture using the hand mixer. Beat the eggs in the separate bowl and whisk them until smooth. When the butter mixture is smooth – start to add the eggs gradually. Mix the butter mixture for 1 min on the medium speed. Then combine the flour and oatmeal together. Add salt and stir it. Add the flour mixture to the butter mixture. After this, sprinkle it with the vanilla extract. Knead the smooth and soft dough. Preheat the air fryer to 360 F. Place the dough into the muffin forms and place them in the air fryer. Cook the muffins for 10 min. Check if the muffins are cooked with the help of the toothpick. Serve the muffins warm!

NUTRITION:

calories 364, fat 27.8, fiber 0.6, carbs 22, protein 6.9

TOFU POTATO SCRAMBLE

Prep time: 15 min | Cooking time: 13 min | Servings: 2

INGREDIENTS:

5 oz tofu	powder
1 sweet potato	1 tsp olive oil
½ tsp canola oil	½ tsp paprika
1 tsp soy sauce	½ tsp dried oregano
¼ tsp garlic	

DIRECTIONS:

Cut tofu into the cubes. Sprinkle tofu cubes with the canola oil and soy sauce. Add garlic powder and shake tofu gently. Leave tofu for 10 min to marinate. Meanwhile, peel the sweet potato and cut it into the same cubes as tofu. Sprinkle the sweet potato with the olive oil, paprika, and dried oregano, Mix it up. Preheat the air fryer to 400 F. Put the sweet potato in the air fryer basket and cook for 8 min. After this, add marinated tofu and cook the meal for 5 min more. When the meal is cooked – shake it well. Then transfer to the serving plates.

NUTRITION:

calories 137, fat 6.7, fiber 3, carbs 14, protein 7.3

CINNAMON FRENCH TOAST

Prep time: 12 min | Cooking time: 10 min | Servings: 2

INGREDIENTS:

2 egg	¼ tsp ground
4 slices white	nutmeg
bread	1 tsp vanilla
1 tbsp sugar	extract
¼ tsp cinna-	2 tbsp milk
mon	1 tbsp maple
¼ tsp ground	syrup
ginger	

DIRECTIONS:

Crack the eggs into the bowl and whisk them well. Then sprinkle the whisked eggs with the cinnamon, ground ginger, ground nutmeg, and vanilla extract. Add milk and sugar. Whisk the mixture until sugar is dissolved. After this, place the bread slices in the egg mixture and leave them until they soak all the egg liquid. Preheat the air fryer to 355 F. Put the bread slices on the rack and cook for 10 min. When the toasts are cooked – serve them immediately.

NUTRITION:

calories 176, fat 5.4, fiber 23.7, carbs 10.8, protein 7.5

VANILLA BREAD PUDDING

Prep time: 15 min | Cooking time: 22 min | Servings: 2

INGREDIENTS:

4 white sand-	3 tsp butter
wich bread	½ tsp ground
slices	cinnamon
1 egg	1 tbsp almond
¼ cup heavy	flakes
cream	2 tsp raisins
1 tsp vanilla	½ tsp olive oil
extract	

DIRECTIONS:

Take off the crust from the sandwich bread slices. Then spread every bread slice with the butter. Spray the ramekin with the olive oil. Place the first bread slice in the ramekin. Then sprinkle it with the vanilla extract. After this, the second bread slice in the ramekin and sprinkle it with the ground cinnamon. Add the third bread slice and sprinkle it with the raisins. Then put the last bread slice in the ramekin. Crack the egg into the bowl and whisk it. Add heavy cream and whisk it. Pour the egg mixture into the ramekin. Sprinkle the pudding mixture with the raisins. Preheat the air fryer to 360 F. Put the ramekin in the air fryer and cook it for 22 min. Serve the cooked pudding immediately.

NUTRITION:

calories 300, fat 16.7, fiber 0.4, carbs 31.7, protein 7.3

MOZZARELLA SAUSAGE STROMBOLI

Prep time: 10 min | Cooking time: 10 min | Servings: 2

INGREDIENTS:

4 oz pizza	cooked, sliced
crust	1 egg yolk
3 oz mozzarel-	¼ tsp cream
la, shredded	1 tsp oregano
3 oz sausages,	

DIRECTIONS:

Roll the pizza crust. Sprinkle the pizza crust with shredded mozzarella. Then add the sliced sausages and sprinkle with the oregano. Roll the pizza crust and secure it in the shape of the crescent. Whisk the egg yolk well and combine it with the cream. Stir it. Then brush the Stromboli with the egg yolk mixture. Preheat the air fryer to 370 F. Put the Stromboli in the air fryer basket and cook it for 10 min. When the Stromboli is cooked – slice it. Taste it!

NUTRITION:
calories 433, fat 23.7, fiber 1.2, carbs 29.4, protein 26.1

STRAWBERRY OATMEAL
Prep time: 10 min | Cooking time: 30 min | Servings: 2

INGREDIENTS:

½ cup milk	1 oz blackberry
1 egg	1 oz strawberry
1 tsp vanilla	1 oz raspberry
extract	1 pinch ground
3 tbsp brown	cinnamon
sugar	1 tsp honey
6 tbsp oatmeal	1 tsp butter
1 pinch salt	

DIRECTIONS:
Crack the egg into the bowl and whisk it. Add the salt, vanilla extract, and milk. Stir it carefully. Then combine the oatmeal and ground cinnamon together. Add the brown sugar and stir it. Combine the blackberries, strawberries, and raspberries in the bowl. Shake them little. Put the oatmeal in the air fryer basket. Then pour the egg mixture and add berries. Preheat the air fryer to 370 F and cook the meal for 30 min. When the oatmeal is cooked – add butter and honey. Mix it up and serve.

NUTRITION:
calories 223, fat 6.6, fiber 3.6, carbs 34.2, protein 7.3

CHEDDAR HASH BROWNS
Prep time: 10 min | Cooking time: 15 min | Servings: 2

INGREDIENTS:

2 potatoes,	powder
baked	3 oz. Cheddar
¼ tsp garlic	cheese, shred-
ded	1 pinch ground
1 tsp butter	black pepper
1 pinch salt	

DIRECTIONS:
Grate the baked potatoes. Preheat the air fryer to 360 F. Toss the butter in the air fryer and melt it. After this, reduce the temperature to 345 F. Put the grated potato in the air fryer basket and cook it for 5 min. After this, stir the grated potato carefully and sprinkle it with the garlic powder, salt, and ground black pepper. Stir the mixture carefully and cook it for 5 min more. After this, sprinkle the mixture with shredded cheese and cook it for 5 min at 365 F. When the hash brown is cooked – stir it carefully with the help of the spatula.

NUTRITION:
calories 318, fat 16.2, fiber 2.4, carbs 31.2, protein 14.2

CHEDDAR BREAD PIZZA
Prep time: 10 min | Cooking time: 4 min | Servings: 2

INGREDIENTS:

1 pitta bread	oregano
3 oz. mozza-	1 tsp pizza
rella cheese,	sauce
shredded	4 slices pepper-
2 oz. Cheddar	oni
cheese, shred-	1 tsp heavy
ded	cream
¼ tsp dried	

DIRECTIONS:
Combine the pizza sauce, heavy cream, and dried oregano in the bowl. Whisk it. Spread the pitta bread with the pizza sauce mixture. Put the pepperoni over the pizza sauce mixture. Then sprinkle it with the shredded mozzarella and Cheddar cheese. Preheat the air fryer to 360 F and put the pizza there. Cook it for 4

min. When the breakfast pizza is cooked – serve it immediately.

NUTRITION:
calories 370, fat 23, fiber 0.7, carbs 16.3, protein 23.9

MOZZARELLA PEPPERONI PATTIES
Prep time: 10 min | Cooking time: 5 min | Servings: 2

INGREDIENTS:

4 thick mozzarella slices	1 egg
	3 tbsp flour
4 pepperoni slices	¼ tsp dried rosemary
3 tbsp panko breadcrumbs	1 pinch salt

DIRECTIONS:
Place the pepperoni slices on two mozzarella slices. Then cover the mozzarella slices with the remaining cheese to make the cheese sandwiches. Beat the egg in the bowl and whisk it. Then sprinkle the mozzarella sandwiches with the flour and dip them in the whisked egg. Sprinkle Mozzarella patties with the panko breadcrumbs. Preheat the air fryer to 400 F. Put the patties in the air fryer basket and cook them for 5 min. Flip them after 2 min of cooking. Serve the patties immediately.

NUTRITION:
calories 329, fat 17.7, fiber 0.8, carbs 18.5, protein 23.8

PAPRIKA SOUFFLÉ
Prep time: 5 min | Cooking time: 5 min | Servings: 2

INGREDIENTS:

3 eggs	¼ tsp paprika
2 tbsp heavy cream	¼ tsp ground turmeric
1 pinch salt	

DIRECTIONS:
Preheat the air fryer to 360 F. Crack the eggs into the bowl and whisk them. Add the heavy cream. Then sprinkle the egg mixture with the salt, paprika, and ground turmeric. Stir it carefully. Pour the egg mixture into 2 ramekins. Put the ramekins in the air fryer basket and cook the soufflé for 5 min. When the soufflé is cooked – chill it for 3 min.

NUTRITION:
calories 148, fat 12.2, fiber 0.2, carbs 1.3, protein 8.7

TABASCO CHICKEN MEATBALLS
Prep time: 10 min | Cooking time: 15 min | Servings: 2

INGREDIENTS:

1 tbsp chives	¼ tsp minced garlic
1 tsp Tabasco	¼ tsp onion powder
5 oz. ground chicken	1 tsp semolina
3 oz. ground pork	1 tsp olive oil

DIRECTIONS:
Take the big bowl and put the ground chicken, ground pork, minced garlic, onion powder, and semolina. Add chives and Tabasco. Stir it carefully. Then make the small meatballs. Preheat the air fryer to 360 F and put the meatballs in the air fryer basket. Cook the meatballs for 15 min. When the meatballs are cooked – let them chill gently.

NUTRITION:
calories 224, fat 9.1, fiber 0.2, carbs 1.7, protein 32

CHEDDAR ZUCCHINI FRITTATA
Prep time: 10 min | Cooking time: 18 min | Servings: 2

INGREDIENTS:

1 zucchini	diced
3 oz. Cheddar cheese, shredded	2 eggs
	2 tbsp milk
	¼ tsp paprika
1 pinch salt	¼ tsp butter
½ white onion,	

DIRECTIONS:

Cut the zucchini into the strips and combine it with the diced onion. Preheat the air fryer to 360 F and toss butter there. When the butter is melted – put the zucchini mixture in the air fryer basket. Cook the zucchini mixture for 8 min. Meanwhile, beat the eggs in the bowl and whisk them. Add the salt, paprika, and milk. Stir it. When the time is over – pour the egg mixture into the air fryer and stir it. Cook the frittata for 5 min at 360 F. Then add the shredded cheese and cook it for 5 min more at 370 F. Serve the cooked frittata immediately.

NUTRITION:

calories 274, fat 19.5, fiber 1.8, carbs 7.6, protein 18.2

MILKY COD

Prep time: 10 min | Cooking time: 13 min | Servings: 2

INGREDIENTS:

10 oz. cod fillet	½ tsp ground black pepper
¼ cup breadcrumbs	½ tsp olive oil
1 egg	1 tsp dried cilantro
¼ cup milk	
1 pinch salt	

DIRECTIONS:

Cut the cod fillet into servings. Then beat the egg into the bowl and whisk it. Add the milk and whisk it for 10 seconds more. After this, sprinkle the cod fillets with the salt, ground black pepper, and dried cilantro. Put the cod fillets in the egg mixture and then coat them with the breadcrumbs. Preheat the air fryer to 360 F. Put the cod fillets in the air fryer and cook the fish for 13 min. Serve the crumbed fish immediately.

NUTRITION:

calories 225, fat 6, fiber 0.8, carbs 11.7, protein 30.9

CHICKEN MUSHROOM ROLLS

Prep time: 10 min | Cooking time: 5 min | Servings: 2

INGREDIENTS:

2 spring roll wraps	2 oz. mushroom
7 oz. chicken breast, cooked	1 oz. onion, diced
1 egg	1 tsp chives
2 oz. carrot	

DIRECTIONS:

Shred the cooked chicken breast. Cut the carrot into the strips. Slice the mushrooms. Combine the shredded chicken breast, carrot strips, and sliced mushrooms in the bowl. Add diced onion and chives. Stir the mixture carefully. Then place the chicken filling into the roll wraps and roll them. Beat the egg in the bowl and whisk it. Seal the spring rolls with the help of the whisked egg. Preheat the air fryer to 360 F. Cook the spring rolls for 5 min. When the meal is cooked – serve it immediately.

NUTRITION:

calories 168, fat 4.8, fiber 1.3, carbs 5.2, protein 25.1

RUNNING CHEDDAR EGGS

Prep time: 5 min | Cooking time: 6 min | Servings: 2

INGREDIENTS:

4 eggs	ded
1 pinch salt	1 tbsp dill,
3 oz. cheddar	chopped
cheese, shred-	¼ tsp butter

DIRECTIONS:

Preheat the air fryer to 360 F. Toss the butter in the air fryer and melt it. Beat the eggs in the melted butter. Sprinkle the eggs with the salt and chopped dill. Cook the eggs for 4 min. After this, sprinkle the eggs with the shredded cheese and cook them for 2 min more. Transfer the cooked eggs to the serving plates.

NUTRITION:

calories 305, fat 23.4, fiber 0.2, carbs 2.1, protein 22

CHEDDAR POTATO HALVES

Prep time: 15 min | Cooking time: 18 min | Servings: 2

INGREDIENTS:

2 potatoes	3 oz. ground
1 tsp scallion,	chicken
chopped	1 tsp tomato
¼ tsp butter	sauce
3 oz. Cheddar	1 pinch salt
cheese, shred-	1 pinch ground
ded	black pepper

DIRECTIONS:

Wash the potatoes carefully and cut them into the halves. Combine the chopped scallions, shredded cheese, ground chicken, tomato sauce, salt, and ground black pepper. Mix the mixture up. After this, remove the flesh from the potato halves and chop it. Combine the potato flesh with the ground chicken mixture. Then fill the potato halves with the chicken mixture. Put the small piece of the butter over every potato halve. Preheat the air fryer to 400 F. Put the potato halves in the air fryer basket and cook them for 18 min. When the potato halves are cooked – the filling should be very soft. Serve the cooked meal immediately.

NUTRITION:

calories 404, fat 17.9, fiber 5.2, carbs 34.2, protein 26.5

CHICKEN STRIPS

Prep time: 10 min | Cooking time: 20 min | Servings: 2

INGREDIENTS:

11 oz. chicken	2 tbsp bread-
fillet	crumbs
¼ tsp salt	¼ tsp ground
¼ tsp dried	black pepper
oregano	1 tsp olive oil
¼ tsp paprika	1 tsp sour
¼ tsp turmeric	cream

DIRECTIONS:

Cut the chicken fillet into the medium strips. Then combine the salt, dried oregano, paprika, turmeric, and ground black pepper in the bowl. Shake it gently to make the homogeneous texture. Then coat the chicken strips with the spice mixture. Combine the sour cream and olive oil together. Whisk it. Sprinkle the chicken strips with the sour cream mixture gently. Then sprinkle the chicken strips with the breadcrumbs. Preheat the air fryer to 360 F. Put the chicken strips in the air fryer basket and cook for 20 min. When the chicken strips are cooked – let them chill and serve.

NUTRITION:

calories 350, fat 14.8, fiber 0.6, carbs 5.6, protein 46.2

WRAPPED BACON EGGS

Prep time: 8 min | Cooking time: 10 min | Servings: 2

INGREDIENTS:

4 eggs, boiled	enne pepper
4 bacon slices	1 pinch paprika
1 pinch salt	½ tsp canola oil
1 pinch cay-	

DIRECTIONS:

Peel the boiled eggs. Sprinkle the bacon slices with the salt, cayenne pepper, and paprika. Preheat the air fryer to 360 F. Put the bacon slices in the air fryer rack and cook for 5 min. After this, chill the bacon. Wrap the peeled eggs in the bacon slices and secure them gently with the toothpicks. After this, put the wrapped eggs in the air fryer basket and sprinkle with the canola oil. Cook the bacon eggs for 5 min more. The eggs are cooked – when the surface of the bacon is a little bit crunchy – the meal is cooked. Serve it!

NUTRITION:

calories 342, fat 25.8, fiber 0.1, carbs 1.4, protein 25.2

BANANA PANCAKES

Prep time: 8 min | Cooking time: 10 min | Servings: 2

INGREDIENTS:

1 tsp flour	2 tsp maple
1 banana	syrup
1 egg	1/3 tsp vanilla
¼ tsp ground	extract
cinnamon	

DIRECTIONS:

Beat the egg in the bowl. Peel the banana and add it to the egg bowl. Mash the egg mixture with the help of the fork. When the mixture is homogenous – add flour and vanilla extract. Mix it up with the help of the hand mixer. Preheat the air fryer to 300 F. Separate the banana mixture into 2 parts. Pour the first part of the banana mixture in the air fryer. Cook it for 5 min. When the pancake is cooked – transfer it to the serving plate. Cook the remaining banana mixture. When 2 pancakes are cooked – serve them with the maple syrup.

NUTRITION:

calories 109, fat 2.4, fiber 1.7, carbs 19.4, protein 3.6

HONEY PUMPKIN MASH

Prep time: 15 min | Cooking time: 11 min | Servings: 2

INGREDIENTS:

1 tbsp honey	10 oz. pumpkin
½ tsp ground	¼ tsp butter
cinnamon	1 tsp heavy
¼ tsp ground	cream
ginger	

DIRECTIONS:

Peel the pumpkin and cut it into the cubes. Sprinkle the pumpkin cubes with the honey and ground cinnamon. Then add ground ginger and shake it. Melt the butter and combine it with the heavy cream. Stir it. Leave the pumpkin cubes for 10 min to let it gives the juice. Preheat the air fryer to 400 F. Put the juicy pumpkin mixture in the air fryer and cook it for 11 min. When the pumpkin is soft – it is cooked. Blend the pumpkin with the help of the hand blender. Then add the melted heavy cream mixture and stir it carefully. Serve the pumpkin mash immediately.

NUTRITION:

calories 95, fat 1.8, fiber 4.5, carbs 20.8, protein 1.7

CHEESE OATMEAL FRITTERS

Prep time: 10 min | Cooking time: 4 min | Servings: 2

INGREDIENTS:

1 egg	1 tbsp brown
10 oz. cottage	sugar
cheese	1 tsp oatmeal
1 tsp semolina	½ tsp vanilla
1 tbsp sour	extract
cream	½ tsp olive oil

DIRECTIONS:

Mash the cottage cheese with the help of the fork. Beat the egg in the mixture and stir it until homogenous. Add semolina, sour cream, brown sugar, oatmeal, and vanilla extract. Mix it up. Then form the medium fritters from the mixture. Preheat the air fryer to 360 F. Spray the air fryer basket with the olive oil inside. Then put the cottage cheese fritters. Cook the fritters for 2 min from each side. When the fritters are cooked – chill for 1 min. Serve the fritters. Sprinkle the meal with the liquid honey if desired.

NUTRITION:

calories 211, fat 7.4, fiber 0.2, carbs 12, protein 22.8

PARMESAN SPINACH QUICHE
Prep time: 15 min | Cooking time: 15 min | Servings: 2

INGREDIENTS:

3 oz. fresh	1 pinch salt
spinach	1 tbsp butter
1 egg	3 oz. Parmesan,
1 tsp cream	shredded
4 tbsp flour	½ tsp dried dill

DIRECTIONS:

Combine the salt, butter, and flour together. Knead the non-sticky dough. Roll the dough with the help of the rolling pin. Then place the rolled dough in the air fryer form. Beat the egg in the bowl and whisk it. Add cream and dried dill. Stir it. Pour the egg mixture into the quiche crust. Chop the fresh spinach and put it in the quiche crust. Preheat the air fryer to 350 F and put the quiche there. Cook the meal for 10 min. After this, sprinkle it with the shredded cheese. Reduce the temperature to 345 F and cook the quiche for 5 min more. Then chill the cooked quiche and serve it.

NUTRITION:

calories 406, fat 21, fiber 1.4, carbs 32, protein 20.7

EGG SANDWICH
Prep time: 10 min | Cooking time: 7 min | Servings: 2

INGREDIENTS:

4 slices of sand-	1 tsp dried dill
wich bread	¼ tsp dried
4 eggs	oregano
1 pinch salt	1 tsp butter

DIRECTIONS:

Make the holes in the sandwich bread slices. Preheat the air fryer to 360 F. Melt the butter and put the bread slices in the air fryer basket. Then beat the eggs in the bread holes. Sprinkle the eggs with the dried dill, salt, and dried oregano. Cook the eggs in holes for 5 min. After this, turn the eggs into holes to another side and cook for 2 min more. Serve the cooked meal hot.

NUTRITION:

calories 285, fat 12.7, fiber 1.2, carbs 29.1, protein 15.2

EGGS IN BACON CUPS
Prep time: 10 min | Cooking time: 12 min | Servings: 2

INGREDIENTS:

1 tbsp scal-	lions, chopped

1 pinch salt	¼ tsp chili
2 eggs	flakes
6 bacon slices	1 tsp butter

DIRECTIONS:

Preheat the air fryer to 360 F. Take the muffin molds and put the better there. After this, place 3 bacon slices in every mold. Then beat the eggs in the molds. Sprinkle the eggs with the chopped scallions and salt. Add chili flakes. Put the bacon cups in the air fryer and cook them for 12 min. When the eggs are cooked – let them chill little. Discard the bacon cups from the muffin molds and serve them.

NUTRITION:

calories 389, fat 30.1, fiber 0.1, carbs 1.4, protein 26.7

LEEK PARMESAN TARTS

Prep time: 10 min | Cooking time: 10 min | Servings: 2

INGREDIENTS:

4 oz. puff pas-try	3 oz. Parmesan, shredded
1 egg yolk	1 pinch salt
¼ tsp ground black pepper	3 oz. leek
¼ tsp chili flakes	½ tsp butter
	1 tsp cream

DIRECTIONS:

Roll the puff pastry. Whisk the egg yolk. Brush the puff pastry with the whisked egg yolk. After this, sprinkle the puff pastry with the shredded cheese. Then sprinkle the ground black pepper, chili flakes, and salt over the shredded cheese. Chop the leek and combine it with the cream. Stir it. Melt butter. Place the chopped leek over the cheese and sprinkle with the butter. Preheat the air fryer to 400 F. Cut the tart into 2 parts and place them in the air fryer. Cook the tarts for

10 min. When the meal is cooked – let it chill little. Serve it!

NUTRITION:

calories 512, fat 34.2, fiber 1.7, carbs 33.7, protein 19.9

AVOCADO EGGS

Prep time: 10 min | Cooking time: 7 min | Servings: 2

Ingredients:

1 avocado, pitted	¼ tsp fresh parsley, chopped
2 eggs	
1 pinch ground black pepper	¼ tsp chives

DIRECTIONS:

Cut the avocado into the halves. Sprinkle the avocado halves with the ground black pepper and chives. Then beat the eggs into the avocado halves. Preheat the air fryer to 360 F. Put the avocado eggs in the air fryer basket and cook them for 7 min. When the meal is cooked – sprinkle it with the chopped fresh parsley. Serve it immediately.

NUTRITION:

calories 268, fat 24, fiber 6.8, carbs 9, protein 7.5

SMOKED SALMON OMELET

Prep time: 10 min | Cooking time: 8 min | Servings: 2

INGREDIENTS:

3 oz. smoked salmon, chopped	¼ tsp ground black pepper
4 eggs	¼ tsp chili flakes
1 tsp scallions	½ tsp butter
1 pinch salt	2 tbsp cream

DIRECTIONS:

Beat the eggs in the bowl and whisk them. Add the scallions and salt. After this, sprinkle the eggs with the ground black pepper, chili flakes, and cream. Stir it carefully. Preheat the air fryer to 360 F. Toss the butter in the air fryer basket and melt it. After this, pour the egg mixture into the melted butter. Add the chopped smoked salmon. Cook the omelet for 8 min. Transfer the cooked omelet onto the serving plates.

NUTRITION:
calories193, fat 12.2, fiber 0.1, carbs 1.3, protein 19

PAPRIKA CHICKEN BUNS
Prep time: 10 min | Cooking time: 12 min | Servings: 2

Ingredients:

6 oz. ground chicken	1 pinch salt
¼ tsp minced garlic	¼ tsp paprika
¼ tsp ground black pepper	4 oz. puff pastry
	½ tsp butter
	1 tbsp water

DIRECTIONS:
Roll the puff pastry. Combine the ground chicken with the minced garlic, ground black pepper, salt, paprika, and butter. Mix the mixture up. After this, cut the puff pastry into 4 squares. Put the ground chicken mixture in the center of every puff pastry square. Secure the edges of the dough to make the shape of the bun. Preheat the air fryer to 370 F. Sprinkle the buns with water and place them in the air fryer basket. Cook the chicken buns for 12 min. When the buns are cooked – let them chill little.

NUTRITION:
calories 484, fat 28.9, fiber 1, carbs 26, protein 28.8

PARMESAN CHORIZO ROLLS
Prep time: 10 min | Cooking time: 11 min | Servings: 2

INGREDIENTS:

3 oz puff pastry	2 oz Parmesan, shredded
3 oz chorizo	
1 tbsp fresh parsley	1 tsp butter
1 tsp tomato sauce	¼ tsp ground thyme

DIRECTIONS:
Roll the puff pastry. Spread it with the tomato sauce and sprinkle it with the shredded cheese. Then chop the fresh parsley put it over the cheese. After this, sprinkle the dough with the ground thyme. Chop the chorizo and add it to the dough too. Roll the dough and cut it into 4 small rolls. Melt the butter. Brush the rolls with the butter. Preheat the air fryer to 365 F. Put the chorizo rolls on the air fryer rack and cook them for 11 min. When the meal is cooked – serve it immediately.

NUTRITION:
calories 537, fat 40.5, fiber 0.8, carbs 21.3, protein 22.6

CHEDDAR CRUMPETS
Prep time: 25 min | Cooking time: 12 min | Servings: 2

INGREDIENTS:

2 oz. Queso Fresco	yeast
2 tbsp milk	¼ tsp butter
3 tbsp flour	2 oz. Cheddar cheese, shredded
¼ tsp sugar	
1 pinch dried	

DIRECTIONS:
Melt Queso Fresco and preheat the milk. Combine the ingredients together and stir until you get the smooth mixture. Then combine flour, sugar, and yeast in the bowl. Start to add the milk

mixture gradually. Stir it constantly. Leave the mixture for 10 min at the warm place. After this, add shredded Cheddar cheese and stir it. Melt the butter and add it to the dough too. Stir it well and leave it for 5 min more. Then pour the smooth dough into the ramekins. Preheat the air fryer to 370 F. Put the ramekins in the air fryer basket and cook for 12 min. When the crumpets are cooked – they will be still soft but with the crunchy surface. Let the crumpets chill little. Serve and

NUTRITION:
calories 209, fat 12.7, fiber 0.4, carbs 10.7, protein 12.7

MAIN DISHES

PORK STRIPS
Prep time: 18 min | Cooking time: 10 min | Servings: 2

INGREDIENTS:

15 oz pork fillet	cider vinegar
1 tsp sesame seeds	1 tsp soy sauce
	1 tsp scallions, chopped
1 tsp sesame oil	½ tsp ground black pepper
1 tsp apple	

DIRECTIONS:
Cut the pork fillet into the strips. Put the pork strips in the bowl and sprinkle them with the sesame oil, apple cider vinegar, soy sauce, and ground black pepper. Mix the meat gently and leave it for 10 min. Preheat the air fryer to 400 F. Put the pork strips in the air fryer basket and cook for 10 min. Shake the pork strips after 6 min of cooking. When the pork strips are cooked – sprinkle them with the chopped scallions and serve.

NUTRITION:
calories 528, fat 30, fiber 0.4, carbs 1, protein 59.7

PINEAPPLE CHICKEN BREAST
Prep time: 15 min | Cooking time: 25 min | Servings: 2

INGREDIENTS:

2 tsp pineapple, canned	black pepper
12 oz chicken breast	½ tsp olive oil
1 tsp butter	1 tbsp mayonnaise
¼ tsp ground	¼ tsp chili flakes

DIRECTIONS:
Make the cut in the chicken breast crosswise. Sprinkle the chicken breast with the ground black

pepper, mayonnaise, and chili flakes. Stir the chicken breast carefully. After this, sprinkle the chicken breast with the olive oil. Chop the pineapple into the tiny pieces. Fill the chicken breast with the chopped pineapple. Add butter and secure the chicken breast with the toothpicks. Preheat the air fryer to 360 F and put the chicken breast in the air fryer basket. Cook the chicken breast for 25 min. When the meal is cooked – let it chill little and slice.

NUTRITION:
calories 252, fat 9.8, fiber 0.1, carbs 2.4, protein 36.2

CATFISH NUGGETS
Prep time: 10 min | Cooking time: 8 min | Servings: 2

INGREDIENTS:

½ cup bread-crumbs	¼ tsp salt
1 egg	2 tbsp cream
12 oz catfish fillet	1 tsp olive oil
	1 tsp dried cilantro

DIRECTIONS:
Crack the egg into the bowl and whisk it. Add cream and stir the egg mixture carefully.After this, cut the catfish fillet into medium pieces. Sprinkle the catfish pieces with the salt and dried oregano. Then dip the fish pieces into the egg mixture. After this, coat the fish pieces in the bread crumbs. Preheat the air fryer to 400 F. Put the chicken nuggets onto the air fryer tray and spray them with the olive oil. Cook the fish nuggets for 8 min. Flip the fish nuggets into another side after 4 min of cooking.

NUTRITION:
calories 396, fat 19.5, fiber 1.2, carbs 20, protein 32.9

CREAMY CORIANDER TILAPIA
Prep time: 12 min | Cooking time: 16 min | Servings: 2

INGREDIENTS:

¼ cup cream	¼ tsp ground coriander
15 oz tilapia fillet	1 tsp fresh thyme
½ tsp garlic, sliced	½ tsp butter

DIRECTIONS:
Put the tilapia fillet in the bowl. Sprinkle it with the sliced garlic, ground coriander, and fresh thyme. Add cream and stir the fish well. Preheat the air fryer to 360 F. Toss the butter in the air fryer basket and melt it. Then put the tilapia fillet in the melted butter. Sprinkle it with the remaining cream mixture and cook for 16 min. Flip the tilapia fillet into another side after 8 min of cooking. Transfer the cooked tilapia to the serving plate.

NUTRITION:
calories 205, fat 4.6, fiber 0.2, carbs 1.5, protein 39.9

ITALIAN BEER COD
Prep time: 20 min | Cooking time: 10 min | Servings: 2

INGREDIENTS:

½ cup beer	crumbs
¼ tsp salt	1 tbsp Italian seasoning
½ tsp ground black pepper	½ tsp olive oil
14 oz cod fillet	1 egg
4 tbsp bread-	

DIRECTIONS:
Sprinkle the cod fillet with the salt and ground black pepper. Then put the cod fillet in the beer and leave it for 10 min. Meanwhile, combine the breadcrumbs and Italian seasoning in

the bowl. Stir the mixture. Crack the egg into the bowl and whisk it. Remove the fish fillet from the beer and cut it into 2 parts. Then dip the fish pieces into the egg mixture. After this, sprinkle the fish pieces with the breadcrumb mixture. Preheat the air fryer to 400 F. Put the fish pieces in the air fryer tray and sprinkle them with the olive oil. Cook the fish fillet for 4 min. After this, flip the fish fillets to another side and cook them for 6 min. Serve the cooked fish immediately.

NUTRITION:
calories 264, fat 7.5, fiber 0.8, carbs 13.1, protein 31.7

GARLIC CATFISH
Prep time: 18 min | Cooking time: 9 min | Servings: 2

INGREDIENTS:

14 oz catfish	½ tsp dried
2 tsp minced	parsley
garlic	1 tsp onion
1 tsp olive oil	powder
½ tsp butter	½ tsp garlic
½ tsp dried dill	powder

DIRECTIONS:
Rub the catfish with the minced garlic. Then combine the olive oil with the dried dill, dried parsley, onion powder, and garlic powder. Whisk it until homogenous. Then brush the catfish with the oil mixture. Leave the catfish for 10 min to marinate. Preheat the air fryer to 400 F. Melt the butter in the air fryer and put the catfish there. Cook the catfish for 6 min. After this, flip the fish to another side and cook for 3 min more. When the fish is cooked – let it chill briefly.

NUTRITION:
calories 494, fat 29.8, fiber 1.6, carbs 18.5, protein 36.4

TURMERIC SNAPPER
Prep time: 20 min | Cooking time: 12 min | Servings: 2

INGREDIENTS:

12 oz snapper	¼ tsp turmeric
½ lemon	½ tsp dried dill
2 garlic cloves	1 tbsp fresh
½ yellow onion	parsley
¼ tsp ground	1 tsp olive oil
thyme	1 tsp butter

DIRECTIONS:
Slice the lemon. Dice the yellow onion and chop the garlic cloves. Rub the snapper with the ground thyme, turmeric, dried dill, and olive oil. Massage the fish gently. After this, fill the snapper with the fresh dill and better. Make the small cuts on the surface of the fish and put the sliced lemon into the cuts. Preheat the air fryer to 365 F. Put the snapper in the air fryer basket and cook the fish for 12 min. Check if the fish is cooked and discard it from the air fryer basket. After this, cut the fish into 2 servings.

NUTRITION:
calories 279, fat 7.4, fiber 1.3, carbs 5.4, protein 44.8

ORANGE BEEF MIGNON
Prep time: 30 min | Cooking time: 18 min | Servings: 2

INGREDIENTS:

15 oz beef mignon	black pepper
	1 tsp olive oil
1 orange	¼ tsp ground
½ tsp white	thyme
pepper	¼ tsp dried
½ tsp ground	cilantro

DIRECTIONS:
Grate the zest from the orange. After this, squeeze juice from the orange. Cut the beef into 2 servings. Combine the orange

juice, orange zest, white pepper, ground black pepper, olive oil, ground thyme, and dried cilantro. Mix it and dip the beef there. Leave the beef for 20 min to marinate in the fridge. Preheat the air fryer to 400 F. Put the beef mignons in the air fryer and sprinkle with ½ part of orange juice mixture. Cook the meat for 18 min. When the beef mignon is cooked – transfer the meal to the serving plates. Taste it.

NUTRITION:
calories 380, fat 17.2, fiber 2.4, carbs 11.2, protein 42

CHICKEN OATMEAL SCHNITZEL
Prep time: 10 min | Cooking time: 13 min | Servings: 2

INGREDIENTS:

2 chicken fillets	1 egg
½ tsp salt	¼ cup oatmeal flour
½ tsp ground black pepper	½ tsp olive oil

DIRECTIONS:
Beat the chicken fillets well. Then sprinkle the chicken fillets with the salt and ground black pepper from each side. Crack the egg into the bowl and whisk it. Dip the chicken fillets in the whisked egg. Then coat the chicken in the oatmeal flour. Preheat the air fryer to 355 F. Put the chicken fillets on the air fryer tray and spray them with the olive oil. Cook the schnitzels for 13 min. Flip the chicken to another side after 6 min of cooking. Serve the cooked schnitzels hot.

NUTRITION:
calories 303, fat 14.9, fiber 2, carbs 20.6, protein 23.2

SALTY PORK BELLY
Prep time: 10 min | Cooking time: 30 min | Servings: 2

Ingredients:

9 oz pork belly	½ tsp ground black pepper
1 tsp salt	
2 tbsp olive oil	

DIRECTIONS:
Sprinkle the pork belly with the salt and ground black pepper. After this, brush the pork belly with the olive oil. Preheat the air fryer to 320 F. Put the pork belly there and cook it for 20 min. After this, increase the temperature to 360 F and cook it for 10 min more. Let the cooked pork belly chill till the room temperature. Taste it!

NUTRITION:
calories 710, fat 48.4, fiber 0.1, carbs 0.3, protein 58.9

RIBEYE BEEF STEAK
Prep time: 10 min | Cooking time: 20 min | Servings: 2

INGREDIENTS:

2 ribeye steak	1 tsp rosemary
1 tsp paprika	1 tbsp Mustard
½ tsp ground black pepper	1 tsp mayonnaise
½ tsp salt	1 tsp olive oil

DIRECTIONS:
Rub the ribeye steaks with the paprika, ground black pepper, salt, rosemary, Mustard, and mayonnaise. Mix the ribeye steaks carefully. After this, sprinkle the meat with the olive oil. Preheat the air fryer to 400 F. Put the ribeye steaks in the air fryer basket and cook for 12 min. Then flip the ribeye steaks to another side and cook for 8 min more at the same temperature.

NUTRITION:
NUTRITION:
calories 736, fat 35.5, fiber 1.6, carbs 3.9, protein 97.4

GARLIC GROUND CHICKEN

Prep time: 10 min | Cooking time: 10 min | Servings: 2

INGREDIENTS:

12 oz ground chicken	flakes
1 tsp minced garlic	½ tsp white pepper
½ tsp onion, grated	1 tsp butter
¼ tsp chili	1 tbsp fresh parsley, chopped

DIRECTIONS:
Take the air fryer tray and put butter there. Preheat the air fryer to 365 F and melt the butter. After this, put the ground chicken in the melted butter. Sprinkle the meat with the minced garlic, grated onion, chili flakes, and white pepper. Stir it and cook the meal for 8 min. After this, stir this meal and sprinkle it with the chopped fresh parsley. Stir the mixture and cook it for 3 min at 400 F. When the meal is cooked – transfer it to the serving plates.

NUTRITION:
calories 345, fat 14.6, fiber 0.3, carbs 1, protein 49.5

PORK CHOPS

Prep time: 10 min | Cooking time: 20 min | Servings: 2

INGREDIENTS:

2 pork chops	black pepper
½ tsp minced garlic	1/3 tsp salt
¼ tsp ground	¼ tsp ground paprika

DIRECTIONS:
Beat the pork chops gently. After this, combine the ground black pepper, salt, and ground paprika in the bowl. Shake it to make homogeneous. Then rub the pork chops with the minced garlic from both sides. Then sprinkle the pork chops with the spices. Preheat the air fryer to 360 F. Cook the pork chops for 20 min. When the time is over – remove the pork chops from the air fryer and serve them.

NUTRITION:
calories 258, fat 19.9, fiber 0.2, carbs 0.5, protein 18.1

CRUNCHY CATFISH

Prep time: 10 min | Cooking time: 10 min | Servings: 2

INGREDIENTS:

12 oz. catfish fillet	ginger
4 tbsp panko breadcrumbs	¼ tsp ground thyme
¼ tsp dried oregano	¼ tsp salt
¼ tsp ground	½ tsp ground paprika
	½ tsp olive oil

DIRECTIONS:
Cut the catfish fillet into 2 parts. Put the panko breadcrumbs in the bowl. Add dried oregano, ground ginger, ground thyme, salt, and ground paprika. Stir the breadcrumb mixture gently. Preheat the air fryer to 350 F. Spray the air fryer basket tray with the olive oil inside. Coat the catfish fillets in the breadcrumb mixture well. Transfer the catfish fillets to the air fryer tray. Cook the fish fillets for 10 min.When the catfish fillets are cooked – transfer them to the serving plates.

NUTRITION:
calories 296, fat 14.9, fiber 1, carbs 10.4, protein 28.4

CELERY CHICKEN WINGS

Prep time: 10 min | Cooking time: 28 min | Servings: 2

INGREDIENTS:

4 chicken wings	celery
1 tbsp corn-starch	1 oz fresh celery root, grated
¼ tsp salt	1 tbsp sour cream
½ tsp garlic, sliced	¼ tsp cayenne pepper
1/3 tsp ground	

DIRECTIONS:

Rub the chicken wings with the sliced garlic, ground celery, grated celery root, sour cream, and cayenne pepper. Mix up the meat and sprinkle the chicken wings with the salt. Mix the meat again. After this, sprinkle the chicken wings with the cornstarch. Shake the chicken wings well. Preheat the air fryer to 400 F. Place the chicken wings in the air fryer tray and cook for 25 min. Then shake the chicken wings well and cook them for 3 min more. Let the cooked chicken wings chill little. Serve the meal!

NUTRITION:

calories 321, fat 12.5, fiber 0.4, carbs 5.6, protein 43.9

ROSEMARY BEEF STEAK

Prep time: 10 min | Cooking time: 20 min | Servings: 2

INGREDIENTS:

1 tbsp fresh rosemary	¼ tsp turmeric
2 beef steaks	1 tsp olive oil
½ tsp salt	¼ tsp cilantro
½ tsp ground black pepper	½ tsp chili flakes
¼ tsp cayenne pepper	1 tsp onion powder

DIRECTIONS:

Chop the fresh rosemary and combine it with the olive oil. Churn it. Take the shallow bowl and combine salt, ground black pepper, cayenne pepper, turmeric, cilantro, chili flakes, and onion flakes together. Shake the bowl well. Then sprinkle the beef steak with the spices generously. After this, rub every steak with the rosemary-oil mixture. Preheat the air fryer to 400 F. Put the beef steaks in the air fryer tray and cook for 10 min. After this, flip the beef steaks to another side and cook the meat for 10 min more. Transfer the cooked beef steak in the serving plates.

NUTRITION:

calories 311, fat 12, fiber 1, carbs 2.7, protein 45.8

CREAMY COD FILLET

Prep time: 10 min | Cooking time: 14 min | Servings: 2

INGREDIENTS:

14 oz cod fillet	1/3 tsp salt
1 tbsp Italian seasoning	¼ tsp turmeric
3 tbsp fresh spinach	½ tsp onion powder
1 tsp butter	1 oz onion, diced
1 tsp cream	

DIRECTIONS:

Wash the spinach carefully and chop it. Melt the butter and combine it with the cream. Churn it. Combine the chopped spinach and cream mixture. Rub the cod fillet with the salt, turmeric, and onion powder. Then sprinkle the cod fillet with Italian seasoning well. After this, combine the diced onion and spinach mixture. Stir it. Put the spinach mixture on the cod fillet. Then sew the cod fillet to make the tube or secure it with the toothpicks. Preheat the air fryer to 355 F. Cook the stuffed cod fillet for 14 min. When the fish is cooked – slice it.

Nutrition: calories 208, fat 5.9, fiber 0.5, carbs 2.9, protein 35.8

BUTTER CHICKEN DRUMSTICKS

Prep time: 10 min | Cooking time: 25 min | Servings: 2

INGREDIENTS:

4 chicken drumsticks
1 tsp minced garlic
¼ tsp red pepper
1 tbsp tomato sauce
1 tsp olive oil
½ tsp ground thyme
½ tsp paprika
½ tsp cayenne pepper
½ tsp mustard powder
½ tsp onion powder

DIRECTIONS:

Take the big bowl and put the minced garlic, red pepper, tomato sauce, olive oil, ground thyme, paprika, cayenne pepper, mustard powder, and onion powder. Stir the mixture with the help of the fork. After this, rub the chicken drumsticks with the spice mixture. Preheat the air fryer to 370 F. Put the chicken drumsticks in the air fryer basket. Cook the meal for 25 min. Shake the chicken drumsticks during the cooking once. Then transfer the chicken drumsticks to the serving plate.

NUTRITION:

calories 194, fat 8.1, fiber 0.9, carbs 3.5, protein 26.1

THYME LAMB RIBS

Prep time: 10 min | Cooking time: 30 min | Servings: 2

INGREDIENTS:

1 tbsp flour
14 oz lamb ribs
1 egg
1 tsp thyme
1 tsp lemon juice
1 tsp cream
1 garlic clove, sliced
1 tbsp canola oil
1 tsp rosemary
½ tsp paprika

DIRECTIONS:

Sprinkle the lamb ribs with the thyme, lemon juice, cream, sliced garlic, canola oil, rosemary, and paprika. Massage the lamb ribs gently. Then crack the egg into the bowl and whisk it. Dip the lamb ribs in the whisked egg. After this, sprinkle the meat with the flour. Preheat the air fryer to 345 F and put the lamb ribs in the air fryer basket. Cook the meal for 25 min. After this, increase the temperature to 370 F and cook the lamb ribs for 5 min more. Let the cooked lamb ribs chill gently.

NUTRITION:

calories 577, fat 36, fiber 0.8, carbs 4.8, protein 55.4

CURRY CHICKEN BREAST

Prep time: 20 min | Cooking time: 10 min | Servings: 2

INGREDIENTS:

15 oz chicken breast
1 tbsp turmeric
1 tsp curry paste
½ yellow onion, diced
1 tbsp mayonnaise
½ tsp onion powder
½ tsp garlic powder
1 tsp butter

DIRECTIONS:

Combine together turmeric, curry paste, sided onion, mayonnaise, onion powder, and garlic powder. Churn the mixture well. Melt the butter and add churned mixture. Stir it. After this, brush the chicken breast with the turmeric mixture and leave it for 10 min. Preheat the air fryer to 380 F. Put the chicken breast in the air fryer basket and cook for 10 min. Flip the chicken breast into another side after 5 min of cooking. Serve the cooked chicken breast immediately.

NUTRITION:
calories 332, fat 11.5, fiber 1.4, carbs 8.2, protein 46.1

MAPLE TURKEY BREAST
Prep time: 10 min | Cooking time: 35 min | Servings: 2

INGREDIENTS:

1 tsp canola oil	1 tsp Dijon mustard
1 tsp ground coriander	2 tbsp maple syrup
½ tsp turmeric	1 tbsp butter
½ tsp onion powder	14 oz turkey breast
½ tsp oregano	
½ tsp salt	

DIRECTIONS:
Combine the canola oil, ground coriander, turmeric, onion powder, oregano, and salt. Churn the mixture to make the spice oil. Brush the turkey breast with the spicy oil. Melt the butter and combine it with the maple syrup, and Dijon mustard. Whisk it. Preheat the air fryer to 360 F and put the turkey breast in the air fryer basket. Cook the turkey breast for 25 min. When the time is over – flip the turkey breast to another side. Sprinkle the turkey breast with the maple syrup mixture generously. Cook the meal for 10 min at 355 F. Let the cooked turkey breast chill little. Slice it.

NUTRITION:
calories 337, fat 4.5, fiber 1.4, carbs 23, protein 34.2

ROSEMARY SALMON STEAK
Prep time: 10 min | Cooking time: 12 min | Servings: 2

INGREDIENTS:

2 salmon steaks	rosemary
½ tsp salt	1 tsp onion powder
½ tsp ground coriander	1 tbsp olive oil
½ tsp dried	

DIRECTIONS:
Sprinkle the salmon steaks with the salt, ground coriander, dried rosemary, and onion powder. Then sprinkle the salmon steaks with the olive oil. Put the salmon steaks in the air fryer basket and cook them for 12 min at 265 F. When the salmon steaks are cooked - serve them immediately.

NUTRITION:
calories 301, fat 18.1, fiber 0.2, carbs 1.2, protein 34.7

STUFFED CALAMARI
Prep time: 15 min | Cooking time: 10 min | Servings: 2

INGREDIENTS:

2 calamari tubes	½ tsp chili flakes
1 red sweet pepper	½ tsp turmeric
1 tbsp fresh dill, chopped	1 tbsp olive oil
½ tsp salt	1 tsp garlic, sliced
	½ tsp butter

DIRECTIONS:
Preheat the air fryer to 400 F. Put the red sweet pepper in the air fryer basket and cook it for 5 min. Then remove the red sweet pepper from the air fryer basket tray and discard the seeds. Chop the red sweet pepper and combine it with the chopped fresh dill. Add sliced garlic and mix it. After this, sprinkle the calamari tubes with the salt, chili flakes, turmeric, and olive oil. Fill the calamari tubes with the red sweet pepper mixture and butter. Secure the calamari tubes with the toothpicks. Preheat the air fryer

to 400 F. Sprinkle the calamari tubes with the olive oil and put in the air fryer basket. Cook the calamari tubes for 5 min. When the meal is cooked – chill it little. Serve it!

<u>NUTRITION</u>:
calories 192, fat 10, fiber 1.2, carbs 8.8, protein 16.1

PAPRIKA CORN BEEF
Prep time: 10 min | Cooking time: 14 min | Servings: 2

<u>INGREDIENTS</u>:

1 cup ground beef	black pepper
1 white onion	½ tsp salt
5 tbsp water	½ tsp ground
½ tsp ground	paprika
	½ tsp butter

<u>DIRECTIONS</u>:
Preheat the air fryer to 400 F. Pour water into the air fryer tray. Peel the onion and slice it. Add the sliced onion in the air fryer tray. Put the tray in the air fryer and cook the onion for 4 min. After this, remove the tray with the onion from the air fryer. Add ground beef. Sprinkle the ground beef with the ground black pepper, salt, ground paprika, and butter. Stir the meat mixture carefully with the help of the fork. Put the tray in the air fryer and cook the corned beef for 10 min at 400 F. Then stir the ground beef mixture carefully and serve it.

<u>NUTRITION</u>:
calories 280, fat 16.1, fiber 1.5, carbs 5.8, protein 27

DIJON TURKEY LEGS
Prep time: 10 min | Cooking time: 30 min
Servings: 2

<u>INGREDIENTS</u>:

2 turkey legs	¼ tsp ground coriander
2 tbsp honey	1 tsp canola oil
½ tsp minced garlic	½ tsp thyme
1 tbsp Dijon mustard	¼ tsp chili pepper

<u>DIRECTIONS</u>:
Combine honey, minced garlic, Dijon mustard, ground coriander, canola oil, thyme, and chili pepper in the mixing bowl. Churn the mixture well. Brush the turkey legs with the sweet mixture generously. Preheat the air fryer to 370 F. Put the turkey legs in the air fryer basket and cook for 30 min. Flip the turkey legs into another side after 15 min of cooking. Then let the cooked turkey legs chill little.

<u>NUTRITION</u>:
calories 239, fat 9.6, fiber 0.4, carbs 18.2, protein 20.3

BEEF ZUCCHINI RINGS
Prep time: 15 min | Cooking time: 13 min | Servings: 2

<u>INGREDIENTS</u>:

1 zucchini	½ tsp garlic powder
6 oz ground beef	¼ tsp salt
½ tsp onion powder	½ tsp paprika
	1 tsp olive oil

<u>DIRECTIONS</u>:
Wash the zucchini carefully and cut it into the thick circles. Then remove the flesh from the zucchini to make the zucchini rings. Combine the ground beef, onion powder, garlic powder, salt, and paprika in the bowl. Stir the meat with the help of the fork. Then fill every zucchini ring with the meat mixture. Sprinkle the zucchini rings with the olive oil. Wrap every zucchini ring in the foil. Preheat the air fryer to 360 F.

Put the zucchini rings in the air fryer basket and cook for 13 min. When the meal is cooked – let it chill for 2-3 min. Then discard the foil. Serve and taste!

NUTRITION:
calories 200, fat 7.9, fiber 1.4, carbs 4.6, protein 27.3

PARMESAN PEPPERS
Prep time: 20 min | Cooking time: 20 min | Servings: 2

INGREDIENTS:

2 sweet yellow peppers	1 tbsp tomato sauce
1 garlic clove, sliced	½ tsp ground black pepper
½ white onion, diced	1 oz Parmesan, shredded
½ tsp salt	1 tsp butter
7 oz ground chicken	½ tsp olive oil

DIRECTIONS:
Pour olive oil into the skillet and preheat it. Then toss the diced onion in the olive oil and sauté it for 2-3 min on the medium heat. Stir it frequently. Discard the seeds from the sweet yellow peppers. Combine the sautéed onion with the sliced garlic, salt, ground chicken, tomato sauce, ground black pepper, and shredded Parmesan cheese. Mix the ground chicken mixture. Fill the sweet yellow peppers with the chicken mixture. Preheat the air fryer to 400 F. Put the butter over every stuffed pepper and transfer them to the air fryer. Cook the stuffed peppers for 20 min. When the meal is cooked – chill it gently and serve.

NUTRITION:
calories 328, fat 13.9, fiber 2.5, carbs 16.1, protein 35.7

CABBAGE BEEF ROLLS
Prep time: 15 min | Cooking time: 20 min | Servings: 2

INGREDIENTS:

2 cabbage leaves	1 tsp sour cream
7 oz ground beef	1 tsp tomato juice
1 egg white	½ tsp olive oil
¼ tsp salt	1 oz carrot, grated
¼ tsp ground black pepper	½ onion, diced
1 tbsp tomato sauce	¼ tsp thyme

DIRECTIONS:
Whisk the egg white gently. Combine the whisked egg white with the ground beef. Sprinkle the meat mixture with salt, ground black pepper, grated carrot, diced onion, and thyme. Stir the meat mixture with the help of the spoon carefully. Separate the meat mixture into two parts. Put the meat mixture on cabbage leaves. Roll every cabbage leaf. Secure the cabbage leaves with the toothpicks if desired. Preheat the air fryer to 360 F. Put the cabbage rolls in the air fryer basket. In the mixing bowl combine the tomato sauce, sour cream, and tomato juice. Add olive oil and whisk it until homogenous. Pour the tomato mixture over the cabbage rolls. Cook the cabbage rolls for 20 min. Flip the cabbage rolls into another side after 1- min of cooking. When the cabbage rolls are cooked- let them chill gently.

NUTRITION:
calories 231, fat 7.9, fiber 1.6, carbs 5.8, protein 32.7

PORK BAK
Prep time: 20 min | Cooking time: 50 min | Servings: 2

INGREDIENTS:

9 oz pork belly
3 cup water
½ tsp onion powder
½ tsp garlic powder
½ tsp ground black pepper
½ tsp cilantro
½ tsp ground ginger
¼ tsp ground cinnamon
½ tsp curry powder
½ tsp salt
1 tsp oregano
1 tsp olive oil
1 bay leaf
2 tsp lemon juice

DIRECTIONS:

Pour water into the saucepan. Put the pork belly and bay leaf in the water and close the lid. Cook the pork belly for 20 min on the medium heat. After this, remove the pork belly from the saucepan and dry it well. Combine the onion powder, garlic powder, ground black pepper, cilantro, ground ginger, ground cinnamon, curry powder, salt, and oregano in the shallow bowl. Stir the mixture. Then rub the dried pork belly with the set of the spices well. After this, combine the lemon juice and olive oil in the bowl and shake it gently. Brush the pork belly with the oil-lemon mixture carefully. Preheat the air fryer to 320 F. Put the pork belly in the air fryer basket and cook it for 30 min more. Turn the pork belly into another side after 15 min of cooking. Slice the cooked pork belly and serve!

NUTRITION:

calories 622, fat 36.9, fiber 1, carbs 2.8, protein 59.4

CHILI PORK SLICES

Prep time: 20 min | Cooking time: 25 min | Servings: 2

INGREDIENTS:

10 oz pork loin
½ carrot, peeled
¼ onion, peeled
¼ tsp salt
½ tsp red pepper
¼ tsp chili flakes
¼ tsp pesto sauce
2 tsp olive oil
1 tsp tomato juice
¼ tsp cayenne pepper

DIRECTIONS:

Preheat an air fryer to 360 F. Chop the carrot and onion into the small pieces. Make as many cuts in the pork loin as you can. Fill the pork loin cuts with the chopped carrot and onion. Combine the olive oil with the salt, red pepper, chili flakes, pesto sauce, olive oil, tomato juice, and cayenne pepper. Mix the mixture. Brush the pork loin with the spicy mixture well and leave it for 10 min to marinate. After this, transfer the pork loin in the air fryer basket. Sprinkle the meat with the remaining spice mixture. Cook the pork loin for 25 min. Flip the pork loin into another side after 10 min of cooking. When the time is over and the meat is cooked – remove it from the air fryer basket. Slice it and serve. Taste it!

NUTRITION:

calories 408, fat 24.8, fiber 1.1, carbs 5.3, protein 39.4

ONION CHICKEN SKIN

Prep time: 15 min | Cooking time: 8 min | Servings: 2

INGREDIENTS:

1 onion, sautéed
4 oz chicken skin, 2 pieces
1 tsp butter
¼ tsp ground black pepper
½ tsp ground paprika
½ tsp oregano
2 oz Cheddar cheese, shredded
½ tsp turmeric
½ tsp olive oil
5 oz ground chicken
½ tsp sour cream

DIRECTIONS:
Combine the ground chicken, turmeric, shredded cheese, sautéed onion, butter, ground black pepper, ground paprika, and oregano. Mix the mixture up. After this, add sour cream and mix it up again. Put the ground chicken mixture on two pieces of the chicken skin. Roll the chicken skin and sew it well. After this, sprinkle the stuffed chicken skin with the olive oil. Preheat the air fryer to 380 F. Put the stuffed chicken skin in the air fryer basket and cook for 8 min. The cooked chicken skin should have crunchy surface. Cook the chicken skin more if you don't get the desired doneness. Let the meal chill little.

NUTRITION:
calories 563, fat 41.2, fiber 1.7, carbs 6.6, protein 40

OREGANO PORK LOAF
Prep time: 15 min | Cooking time: 15 min | Servings: 2

INGREDIENTS:

1 tbsp tomato sauce	½ tsp turmeric
13 oz minced pork	½ tsp onion powder
1 egg	½ tsp garlic powder
1 tsp dried oregano	¼ tsp cayenne pepper
½ tsp thyme	1 tsp semolina
½ tsp salt	1 tsp butter

DIRECTIONS:
Take the big mixing bowl and put there the minced pork, dried oregano, thyme, salt, turmeric, onion powder, garlic powder, cayenne pepper, and semolina. Beat the egg in the minced pork mixture and mix it up. Make the shape of the loaf from the minced pork mixture. Preheat the air fryer to 370 F. Melt the butter in the air fryer basket. After this, put the pork loaf in the melted butter. Cook the pork loaf for 15 min. When the pork loaf is cooked – let it chill well. Sprinkle the meatloaf with the tomato sauce. After this, slice the pork loaf and serve.

NUTRITION:
calories 330, fat 10.8, fiber 0.9, carbs 4, protein 51.7

TENDER BEEF BURGERS
Prep time: 15 min | Cooking time: 17 min | Servings: 2

INGREDIENTS:

½ tsp lemon zest	rosemary
13 oz ground beef	½ tsp dried dill
1/3 tsp ground black pepper	½ tsp olive oil
½ tsp salt	¼ onion, diced
¼ tsp dried	½ tsp minced garlic
	¼ tsp cayenne pepper

DIRECTIONS:
Preheat the air fryer to 370 F. Put the ground beef in the bowl. Sprinkle the ground beef with the lemon zest, ground black pepper, salt, dried rosemary, dried dill, diced onion, minced garlic, and cayenne pepper. Mix the ground beef mixture with the help of the fingertips. Make the medium burgers from the ground beef mixture. Pour the olive oil into the air fryer basket. Then put the beef burgers in the olive oil. Cook the meal for 17 min. Do not stir the burgers during the cooking. When the burgers are cooked – serve them immediately.

NUTRITION:
calories 362, fat 12.7, fiber 0.6, carbs 2.2, protein 56.2

HONEY PORK MEATBALLS

Prep time: 15 min | Cooking time: 16 min | Servings: 2

INGREDIENTS:

1 tsp honey	½ tsp oregano
10 oz ground pork	¼ tsp salt
1 tsp onion powder	1 tbsp tomato sauce
¼ tsp butter	½ tbsp flour
½ tsp dried cilantro	½ tsp olive oil
	½ tsp ground ginger

DIRECTIONS:

Put the ground pork in the bowl. Sprinkle the meat with the onion powder, butter, dried cilantro, oregano, salt, flour, and ground ginger. Mix the ground pork mixture carefully. Preheat the air fryer to 360 F. Sprinkle the air fryer basket with the olive oil. Then make the small meatballs from the ground pork mixture. Cook the meatballs in the olive oil for 10 min. Meanwhile, combine the honey and tomato sauce. Then brush the meatballs with the honey sauce. Cook the meatballs for 6 min more. Then let the meatballs chill gently. Serve the meal!

NUTRITION:

calories 243, fat 6.7, fiber 0.5, carbs 6.3, protein 37.6

CHEDDAR CHICKEN BREAST

Prep time: 15 min | Cooking time: 18 min | Servings: 2

INGREDIENTS:

1 ham slices	1 tsp fresh parsley, chopped
1/3 tsp ground black pepper	
12 oz chicken breast, skinless, boneless	¼ tsp salt
	¼ tsp chili flakes
2 slices Cheddar cheese	1 tsp salsa sauce

½ tsp olive oil

DIRECTIONS:

Make the crosswise cut in the chicken breast. Sprinkle the chicken breast with the ground black pepper, salt, chili flakes, and salsa sauce. Massage the chicken breast gently. Then put the ham slices and cheese slices in the chicken cut. Secure the chicken breast with the toothpicks. Then sprinkle the chicken breast with the olive oil. Preheat the air fryer to 370 F. Put the chicken breast in the air fryer basket and cook for 18 min. When the chicken breast is cooked – pin it with the help of the knife. If the juice from the chicken is clear – it is cooked. Serve the chicken breast hot.

NUTRITION:

calories 341, fat 15.9, fiber 0.3, carbs 1.4, protein 45.5

GARLIC PORK SATAY

Prep time: 30 min | Cooking time: 14 min | Servings: 2

INGREDIENTS:

10 oz pork chops	sauce
	1 tsp canola oil
½ tsp garlic clove, sliced	2 oz shallot, chopped
½ tsp chili paste	4 tsp coconut milk
1 tbsp soy	

DIRECTIONS:

Preheat the air fryer to 360 F. Chop the pork chops into the satay pieces. Place the pork satay pieces in the bowl. Sprinkle the meat with the sliced garlic, chili paste, soy sauce, and chopped shallot. Mix the meat mixture carefully with the help of the fingertips. Leave the meat for 20 min to marinate. Then sprinkle the air fryer basket with the olive oil. Put the marinated meat in the air fryer and cook for 13 min. Stir the meat 3 times during the cooking. The cooked meat should be golden brown. Then sprinkle the meat with the coconut milk and cook it for 1 min more. Shake the meat and skewer it on the skewers. Serve the pork satay hot.

<u>NUTRITION</u>:
calories 621, fat 48.2, fiber 1.2, carbs 9.8, protein 37.4

GINGER PAPRIKA SHRIMPS
Prep time: 15 min | Cooking time: 5 min | Servings: 2

<u>INGREDIENTS</u>:

4 tiger Royal shrimps	½ tsp garlic clove, minced
½ tsp ground ginger	¼ tsp sriracha
1 tsp paprika	½ tsp soy sauce
1 tsp olive oil	¼ tsp peanut butter

<u>DIRECTIONS</u>:
Peel the shrimps. Melt the peanut butter. Combine the melted butter with the ground ginger, paprika, olive oil, minced garlic clove, sriracha, and soy sauce. Churn the mixture well. Then dip the shrimps in the peanut butter mixture. Leave the shrimps for 10 min to marinate. After this, preheat the air fryer to 400 F. Put the shrimps in the air fryer basket and sprinkle with the remaining peanut butter sauce. Cook the shrimps for 5 min. After this, shake the shrimps well. Serve the meal hot.

<u>NUTRITION</u>:
calories 185, fat 4.8, fiber 0.5, carbs 1.5, protein 34.5

TOMATO BEEF
Prep time: 15 min | Cooking time: 25 min | Servings: 2

<u>INGREDIENTS</u>:

1 tomato	sauce
10 oz ground beef	1 tsp tomato juice
1 tsp fresh thyme	½ yellow onion, diced
½ tsp ground black pepper	¼ tsp ground bay leaf
1 tbsp fresh parsley, chopped	1/3 tsp salt
1 tsp tomato	1 tsp sour cream

<u>DIRECTIONS</u>:
Wash the tomato and chop it. Put the chopped tomato in the blender. Add fresh thyme, chopped fresh parsley, ground black pepper, tomato sauce, tomato juice, salt, and sour cream. Blend the mixture until smooth. Sprinkle the smooth tomato mixture with the ground bay leaf and diced onion. Then combine together the ground beef and tomato mixture. Mix it with the help of the spatula. Preheat the air fryer to 360 F. Put the ground beef mixture in the air fryer tray. Cook the meal for 25 min. Stir the ground beef after 10 min of cooking. When the meal is cooked – stir it again.

<u>NUTRITION</u>:
calories 289, fat 9.4, fiber 1.4, carbs 5, protein 43.9

CAYENNE LAMB STEAK
Prep time: 20 min | Cooking time: 30 min | Servings: 2

<u>INGREDIENTS</u>:

2 lamb steaks	1 tbsp apple cider vinegar
½ tsp cayenne pepper	1 tsp olive oil
½ tsp ground black pepper	½ tsp minced garlic
½ tsp salt	½ tsp dried rosemary
½ tsp lemon zest	

DIRECTIONS:

Beat the lamb steak gently. Combine the cayenne pepper, ground black pepper, salt, lemon zest, olive oil, minced garlic, and dried rosemary. Churn the mixture well. After this, sprinkle the lamb steaks with the apple cider vinegar. Rub the lamb steaks with the olive oil mixture and leave for 10 min to marinate. Preheat the air fryer to 330 F. Put the lamb steaks in the air fryer basket. Cook the lamb steaks for 15 min. After this, flip the lamb steaks to another side and cook the meat for 15 min more. When the lamb steaks are cooked – transfer them to the serving plates.

NUTRITION:

calories 217, fat 9.5, fiber 0.4, carbs 1.2, protein 29.6

ROSEMARY LAMB SHANK

Prep time: 20 min | Cooking time: 15 min | Servings: 2

INGREDIENTS:

15 oz lamb shank	flakes
1 tsp dried rosemary	1 tsp apple cider vinegar
½ tsp salt	1 tsp canola oil
¼ lime	½ tsp ground ginger
½ tsp chili	½ tsp oregano

DIRECTIONS:

Squeeze the juice from the lime. Combine the lime juice with the dried rosemary, salt, chili flakes, apple cider vinegar, canola oil, ground ginger, and oregano. Stir the spices gently. Sprinkle the lamb shank with the spicy mixture and leave it for 15 min to let the meat soaks the spices. Preheat the air fryer to 400 F. Put the lamb shank in the air fryer basket. Then sprinkle the lamb shank with the remaining spice mixture. Cook the lamb shank for 15 min. Shake the lamb shank after 8 min of cooking. When the lamb shank is cooked – let it chill little.

NUTRITION:

calories 425, fat 18.1, fiber 0.7, carbs 1.9, protein 59.9

YOGURT CHICKEN KEBAB

Prep time: 15 min | Cooking time: 10 min | Servings: 2

INGREDIENTS:

12 oz chicken fillet	2 tbsp Plain yogurt
1 tsp curry powder	½ tsp salt
½ tsp garlic powder	½ tsp ground paprika
½ tsp onion powder	¼ tsp chili flakes

DIRECTIONS:

Cut the chicken fillet into the cubes. Combine Plain yogurt with the curry powder, garlic powder, onion powder, salt, chili flakes, and ground paprika. Whisk it carefully. Then dip the chicken cubes in the yogurt mixture. Preheat the air fryer to 360 F. Put the chicken cubes in the air fryer basket. Cook the chicken kebabs for 10 min. When the time is over – shake the chicken kebabs gently. Transfer the meal to the serving plates.

NUTRITION:

calories 343, fat 13, fiber 0.6, carbs 3, protein 50.5

DIJON CHICKEN

Prep time: 10 min | Cooking time: 12 min | Servings: 2

INGREDIENTS:

12 oz chicken breast, skinless, boneless,	chopped 2 tsp curry paste

1 tsp Dijon	sliced
mustard	½ tsp olive oil
1 tsp minced	¼ cup milk
garlic	¼ cup chicken
1 yellow onion,	stock

DIRECTIONS:

Preheat the air fryer to 380 F. Put the chopped chicken in the air fryer basket. Then add the sliced onion. After this, sprinkle the chicken with the Dijon mustard, minced garlic, olive oil, and milk. Combine the curry paste and chicken stock in the bowl and whisk it. When the curry paste is dissolved – pour the liquid into the air fryer basket. Stir the chicken gently using the wooden spatula. Cook the curry chicken for 12 min. After this, stir the curry chicken gently and serve it.

NUTRITION:

calories 280, fat 9.2, fiber 1.3, carbs 8.7, protein 38.2

PORK RIBS

Prep time: 15 min | Cooking time: 12 min | Servings: 2

INGREDIENTS:

13 oz pork ribs	1 tsp olive oil
1 tsp cornstarch	1 tsp apple
1 tsp soy sauce	cider vinegar
1 tsp honey	½ tsp butter
½ tsp tomato	½ tsp dried
sauce	rosemary
½ tsp garlic,	½ tsp ground
sliced	ginger

DIRECTIONS:

Put the pork ribs in the bowl. Sprinkle the pork ribs with the soy sauce, honey, tomato sauce, sliced garlic, olive oil, apple cider vinegar, dried rosemary, and ground ginger. Mix the pork ribs gently. After this, preheat the air fryer to 400 F. Sprinkle the pork ribs with the cornstarch and shake them. Toss the butter in the air fryer basket. Melt the butter and add the pork ribs. Cook the pork ribs for 12 min. Shake the pork ribs in 5 min. When the pork ribs are cooked – they will be a little bit crunchy. Transfer the meal to the serving plates.

NUTRITION:

calories 347, fat 4.7, fiber 4.5, carbs 45.3, protein 35.1

COCONUT CHILI BEEF STRIPS

Prep time: 20 min | Cooking time: 16 min | Servings: 2

INGREDIENTS:

1 tsp chili pepper	1 tsp butter
¼ tsp sriracha	½ tsp dried
2 tsp coconut	rosemary
milk	14 oz beef tenderloin
1 tsp peanut	½ tsp sage
butter	

DIRECTIONS:

Cut the beef tenderloin into the strips. Put the beef strips in the bowl. Sprinkle the beef strips with the chili pepper, sriracha, coconut milk, peanut butter, butter, dried rosemary, and sage. Mix the beef strips with the help of the fingertips.After this, leave the beef strips for 10 min in the fridge to marinate. Preheat the air fryer to 400 F. Put the beef strips in the air fryer basket. Cook the beef strips for 10 min. The shake the beef strips and cook for 6 min more. When the beef strips are cooked – chill them till the room temperature.

NUTRITION:

calories 456, fat 22.7, fiber 0.6, carbs 1.5, protein 58.3

OAT CHICKEN SAUSAGES

Prep time: 25 min | Cooking time: 10 min | Servings: 2

INGREDIENTS:

10 oz ground chicken	1 tsp butter
½ tsp garlic powder	½ tsp dried dill
1 tsp onion, grated	1 egg white
½ tsp salt	1 tsp sour cream
	1 tsp oatmeal
	¼ tsp canola oil

DIRECTIONS:

Whisk the egg white and pour it into the bowl. Add ground chicken, garlic powder, grated onion, salt, and dried dill. Then add oatmeal. Melt the butter and add it to the ground chicken. Add sour cream and mix the chicken mixture. Then form the medium sausages and place them in them in the freezer for 10 min. Preheat the air fryer to 400 F. Sprinkle the frozen chicken sausages with the canola oil and place them in the air fryer basket. Cook the chicken sausages for 5 min on each side. When the sausages are cooked – serve them hot.

NUTRITION:

calories 311, fat 13.5, fiber 0.2, carbs 1.6, protein 43.2

PARMESAN SWEET POTATO CASSEROLE

Prep time: 15 min | Cooking time: 35 min | Servings: 2

INGREDIENTS:

2 sweet potatoes, peeled	2 oz Parmesan cheese, shredded
½ yellow onion, sliced	½ tsp salt
½ cup cream	1 tomato
¼ cup spinach	1 tsp olive oil

DIRECTIONS:

Chop the sweet potatoes. Chop the tomato. Chop the spinach. Spray the air fryer tray with the olive oil. Then place on the layer of the chopped sweet potato. Add the layer of the sliced onion. After this, sprinkle the sliced onion with the chopped spinach and tomatoes. Sprinkle the casserole with the salt and shredded cheese. Pour cream. Preheat the air fryer to 390 F. Cover the air fryer tray with the foil. Cook the casserole for 35 min. When the casserole is cooked – serve it.

NUTRITION:

calories 93, fat 1.8, fiber 3.4, carbs 20.3, protein 1.8

SPICY ZUCCHINI SLICES

Prep time: 10 min | Cooking time: 6 min | Servings: 2

INGREDIENTS:

1 tsp cornstarch	1 tbsp flour
1 zucchini	1 egg
½ tsp chili flakes	¼ tsp salt

DIRECTIONS:

Slice the zucchini and sprinkle with the chili flakes and salt. Crack the egg into the bowl and whisk it. Dip the zucchini slices in the whisked egg. Combine to-gether cornstarch with the flour. Stir it. Coat the zucchini slices with the cornstarch mixture. Pre-heat the air fryer to 400 F. Place the zucchini slices in the air fryer tray. Cook the zucchini slices for 4 min. After this, flip the slices to another side and cook for 2 min more. Serve the zucchini slices hot.

<u>NUTRITION</u>:
calories 67, fat 2.4, fiber 1.2, carbs 7.7, protein 4.4

CHEDDAR POTATO GRATIN
Prep time: 15 min | Cooking time: 20 min | Servings: 2

<u>INGREDIENTS</u>:

2 potatoes
1/3 cup half and half
1 tbsp oatmeal flour

1/4 tsp ground black pepper
1 egg
2 oz Cheddar cheese

<u>DIRECTIONS</u>:
Wash the potatoes and slice them into thin pieces. Preheat the air fryer to 365 F. Put the potato slices in the air fryer and cook them for 10 min. Meanwhile, combine the half and half, oatmeal flour, and ground black pepper. Crack the egg into the liquid and whisk it carefully. Shred Cheddar cheese. When the potato is cooked – take 2 ramekins and place the pota-toes on them. Pour the half and half mixture. Sprinkle the gratin with shredded Cheddar cheese. Cook the gratin for 10 min at 360 F. Serve the meal immediately.

<u>NUTRITION</u>:
calories 353, fat 16.6, fiber 5.4, carbs 37.2, protein 15

SALTY LEMON ARTICHOKES
Prep time: 15 min | Cooking time: 45 min | Servings: 2

<u>INGREDIENTS</u>:

1 lemon
2 artichokes
1 tsp kosher

salt
1 garlic head
2 tsp olive oil

<u>DIRECTIONS</u>:
Cut off the edges of the arti-chokes. Cut the lemon into the halves. Peel the garlic head and chop the garlic cloves roughly. Then place the chopped garlic in the artichokes. Sprinkle the artichokes with the olive oil and kosher salt. Then squeeze the lemon juice into the artichokes. Wrap the artichokes in the foil. Preheat the air fryer to 330 F. Place the wrapped artichokes in the air fryer and cook for 45 min. When the artichokes are cooked – discard the foil and serve.

<u>NUTRITION</u>:
calories 133, fat 5, fiber 9.7, carbs 21.7, protein 6

ASPARAGUS & PARMESAN
Prep time: 10 min | Cooking time: 6 min | Servings: 2

<u>INGREDIENTS</u>:

1 tsp sesame oil
11 oz aspara-gus
1 tsp chicken

stock
1/2 tsp ground white pepper
3 oz Parmesan

<u>DIRECTIONS</u>:
Wash the asparagus and chop it roughly. Sprinkle the chopped asparagus with the chicken stock and ground white pepper. Then sprinkle the vegetables with the sesame oil and shake them. Place the asparagus in the air fryer basket. Cook the vegetables for 4 min at 400 F. Meanwhile, shred Parmesan cheese. When the time is over – shake the aspar-agus gently and sprinkle with the shredded cheese. Cook the

asparagus for 2 min more at 400 F. After this, transfer the cooked asparagus in the serving plates.

calories 189, fat 11.6, fiber 3.4, carbs 7.9, protein 17.2

CARROT LENTIL BURGERS
Prep time: 10 min | Cooking time: 12 min | Servings: 2

INGREDIENTS:

6 oz lentils, cooked	1 tsp semolina
1 egg	½ tsp salt
2 oz carrot, grated	1 tsp turmeric
	1 tbsp butter

DIRECTIONS:
Crack the egg into the bowl and whisk it. Add the cooked lentils and mash the mixture with the help of the fork. Then sprinkle the mixture with the grated carrot, semolina, salt, and turmeric. Mix it up and make the medium burgers. Put the butter into the lentil burgers. It will make them juicy. Preheat the air fryer to 360 F. Put the lentil burgers in the air fryer and cook for 12 min. Flip the burgers into another side after 6 min of cooking. Then chill the cooked lentil burgers and serve them.

NUTRITION:
calories 404, fat 9, fiber 26.9, carbs 56, protein 25.3

CORN ON COBS
Prep time: 10 min | Cooking time: 10 min | Servings: 2

INGREDIENTS:

2 fresh corn on cobs	1 tsp salt
2 tsp butter	1 tsp paprika
	¼ tsp olive oil

DIRECTIONS:
Preheat the air fryer to 400 F. Rub the corn on cobs with the salt and paprika. Then sprinkle the corn on cobs with the olive oil. Place the corn on cobs in the air fryer basket. Cook the corn on cobs for 10 min. When the time is over – transfer the corn on cobs in the serving plates and rub with the butter gently. Serve the meal immediately.

NUTRITION:
calories 122, fat 5.5, fiber 2.4, carbs 17.6, protein 3.2

SUGARY CARROT STRIPS
Prep time: 10 min | Cooking time: 10 min | Servings: 2

INGREDIENTS:

2 carrots	sauce
1 tsp brown sugar	1 tsp honey
1 tsp olive oil	½ tsp ground black pepper
1 tbsp soy	

DIRECTIONS:
Peel the carrot and cut it into the strips. Then put the carrot strips in the bowl. Sprinkle the carrot strips with the olive oil, soy sauce, honey, and ground black pepper. Shake the mixture gently. Preheat the air fryer to 360 F. Cook the carrot for 10 min. After this, shake the carrot strips well.

NUTRITION:
calories 67, fat 2.4, fiber 1.7, carbs 11.3, protein 1.1

ONION GREEN BEANS
Prep time: 10 min | Cooking time: 12 min | Servings: 2

INGREDIENTS:

11 oz green beans	powder
1 tbsp onion	1 tbsp olive oil
	½ tsp salt

¼ tsp chili flakes

DIRECTIONS:
Wash the green beans carefully and place them in the bowl. Sprinkle the green beans with the onion powder, salt, chili flakes, and olive oil. Shake the green beans carefully. Preheat the air fryer to 400 F. Put the green beans in the air fryer and cook for 8 min. After this, shake the green beans and cook them for 4 min more at 400 F. When the time is over – shake the green beans. Serve the side dish and

NUTRITION:
calories 1205, fat 7.2, fiber 5.5, carbs 13.9, protein 3.2

MOZZARELLA RADISH SALAD
Prep time: 10 min | Cooking time: 20 min | Servings: 2

INGREDIENTS:

8 oz radish	½ tsp salt
4 oz Mozzarella	1 tbsp olive oil
1 tsp balsamic vinegar	1 tsp dried oregano

DIRECTIONS:
Wash the radish carefully and cut it into the halves. Preheat the air fryer to 360 F. Put the radish halves in the air fryer basket. Sprinkle the radish with the salt and olive oil. Cook the radish for 20 min. Shake the radish after 10 min of cooking. When the time is over – transfer the radish to the serving plate. Chop Mozzarella roughly. Sprinkle the radish with Mozzarella, balsamic vinegar, and dried oregano. Stir it gently with the help of 2 forks. Serve it immediately.

NUTRITION:
calories 241, fat 17.2, fiber 2.1, carbs 6.4, protein 16.9

CREMINI MUSHROOM SATAY
Prep time: 10 min | Cooking time: 6 min | Servings: 2

INGREDIENTS:

7 oz cremini mushrooms	½ tsp balsamic vinegar
2 tbsp coconut milk	½ tsp curry powder
1 tbsp butter	½ tsp white pepper
1 tsp chili flakes	

DIRECTIONS:
Wash the mushrooms carefully. Then sprinkle the mushrooms with the chili flakes, curry powder, and white pepper. Preheat the air fryer to 400 F. Toss the butter in the air fryer basket and melt it. Put the mushrooms in the air fryer and cook for 2 min. Shake the mushrooms well and sprinkle with the coconut milk and balsamic vinegar. Cook the mushrooms for 4 min more at 400 F. Then skewer the mushrooms on the wooden sticks and serve.

NUTRITION:
calories 116, fat 9.5, fiber 1.3, carbs 5.6, protein 3

EGGPLANT RATATOUILLE
Prep time: 15 min | Cooking time: 15 min | Servings: 2

INGREDIENTS:

1 eggplant	½ tsp garlic clove, sliced
1 sweet yellow pepper	1 tsp olive oil
3 cherry tomatoes	½ tsp ground black pepper
1/3 white onion, chopped	½ tsp Italian seasoning

DIRECTIONS:
Preheat the air fryer to 360 F. Peel the eggplants and chop them.

Put the chopped eggplants in the air fryer basket. Chop the cherry tomatoes and add them to the air fryer basket. Then add chopped onion, sliced garlic clove, olive oil, ground black pepper, and Italian seasoning. Chop the sweet yellow pepper roughly and add it to the air fryer basket. Shake the vegetables gently and cook for 15 min. Stir the meal after 8 min of cooking. Transfer the cooked ratatouille in the serving plates.

NUTRITION:
calories 149, fat 3.7, fiber 11.7, carbs 28.9, protein 5.1

CHEDDAR PORTOBELLO MUSHROOMS
Prep time: 15 min | Cooking time: 6 min | Servings: 2

INGREDIENTS:

2 Portobello mushroom hats	½ tsp ground black pepper
2 slices Cheddar cheese	1 egg
¼ cup panko breadcrumbs	1 tsp oatmeal
½ tsp salt	2 oz bacon, chopped cooked

DIRECTIONS:
Crack the egg into the bowl and whisk it. Combine the ground black pepper, oatmeal, salt, and breadcrumbs in the separate bowl. Dip the mushroom hats in the whisked egg. After this, coat the mushroom hats in the breadcrumb mixture. Preheat the air fryer to 400 F. Place the mushrooms in the air fryer basket tray and cook for 3 min. After this, put the chopped bacon and sliced cheese over the mushroom hats and cook the meal for 3 min.

NUTRITION:
calories 376, fat 24.1, fiber 1.8, carbs 14.6, protein 25.2

CREAMY CAULIFLOWER HEAD
Prep time: 10 min | Cooking time: 17 min | Servings: 2

INGREDIENTS:

12 oz cauliflower head	black pepper
2 tbsp cream	1 tsp turmeric
1 tbsp flour	1 tsp salt
½ tsp ground	1 tsp olive oil

DIRECTIONS:
Wash the cauliflower head carefully. Combine the cream and flour in the bowl. Add ground black pepper and turmeric. Whisk the mixture. Then sprinkle the cauliflower head with the cream mixture. Let the cauliflower soaks the cream. Sprinkle the cauliflower with salt. Preheat the air fryer to 360 F. Put the cauliflower head in the air fryer tray. Cook the vegetables for 12 min. After this, sprinkle the cauliflower with the olive oil. Cook the cauliflower head for 5 min at 390 F. When the cauliflower is cooked – it will have the light brown crusted surface. Serve it and

NUTRITION:
calories 90, fat 3.3, fiber 4.7, carbs 13.4, protein 4

CREAM CHEESE BAKED POTATO
Prep time: 15 min | Cooking time: 22 min | Servings: 2

INGREDIENTS:

1 tsp cream cheese	téed
2 potatoes	1 oz sweet peas, cooked
½ tsp salt	1 tsp butter
½ tsp white pepper	½ tsp minced garlic
½ onion, sau-	

DIRECTIONS:
Preheat the air fryer to 365 F. Wash the potatoes carefully and place them in the air fryer basket. Cook the potatoes for 18 min. Meanwhile, churn together the cream cheese, minced garlic, and white pepper. Add the sautéed onion and sweet peas. Add salt and mix the mixture up. After this, melt the butter. When the time is over – remove the baked potatoes from the air fryer and cut them into the halves. Scoop the flesh from the potatoes gently. Combine the potato flesh and cream cheese mixture together. Then fill the potato halves with the cream cheese mixture. Put the potatoes in the air fryer. Cook the meal for 4 min at 400 F. When the potatoes are cooked – let them chill gently.

NUTRITION:
calories 195, fat 2.8, fiber 6.6, carbs 38.7, protein 4.9

CAYENNE PEPPER BRUSSEL SPROUTS
Prep time: 10 min | Cooking time: 15 min | Servings: 2

INGREDIENTS:

1 tbsp butter	stock
10 oz Brussel sprouts	1 tsp paprika
½ tsp cayenne pepper	½ tsp lemon juice
4 tbsp chicken	¼ tsp salt

DIRECTIONS:
Cut Brussel sprouts into the halves. Churn the butter with the cayenne pepper and paprika. Add salt and stir it carefully. Then sprinkle Brussel sprouts halves with the lemon juice. Preheat the air fryer to 380 F. Put the butter mixture in the air fryer basket. Melt the butter and add Brussel sprouts halves. Cook the vegetables for 15 min. Shake the vegetables after 7 min of cooking. Then let the cooked vegetables chill gently.

NUTRITION:
calories 118, fat 6.5, fiber 5.8, carbs 13.9, protein 5.2

BELL PEPPER SLICES
Prep time: 20 min | Cooking time: 10 min | Servings: 2

INGREDIENTS:

1 sweet red pepper	1 tsp olive oil
	½ tsp dried dill
1 yellow sweet pepper	½ tsp dried parsley
1 garlic clove	1 tsp butter
1 tbsp apple cider vinegar	1 pinch salt

DIRECTIONS:
Wash the sweet peppers carefully and discard seeds. Slice the sweet peppers. Preheat the air fryer to 400 F. Toss the butter in the air fryer basket and melt it. Then add the sweet peppers slices. Cook the sweet peppers for 10 min. Shake them well after 5 min of cooking. Meanwhile, peel the garlic clove and slice it. Combine the sliced garlic with the apple cider vinegar and olive oil. Add dried dill and dried parsley. Sprinkle the mixture with the pinch of salt and whisk it well. When the peppers are cooked – let the chill till the room temperature. Then sprinkle the sweet peppers with the oily mixture well. Put the meal in the fridge for 10 min. Serve it!

NUTRITION:
calories 86, fat 4.6, fiber 1.7, carbs 11.1, protein 1.7

SUGARY PUMPKIN WEDGES
Prep time: 15 min | Cooking time: 8 min | Servings: 2

INGREDIENTS:

1 tsp raisins	5 tbsp water
12 oz pumpkin	2 tbsp brown
1 tsp ground	sugar
cinnamon	1 tsp fresh gin-
1 tsp butter	ger, grated

DIRECTIONS:

Peel the pumpkin and cut it into the serving wedges. Melt the butter and combine it together with the ground cinnamon, brown sugar, and grated ginger. Churn the mixture gently. Rub every pumpkin wedge with the butter mixture well. Leave it. Preheat the air fryer to 390 F. Pour water into the air fryer basket. Add raisins and pumpkin wedges. After this, add all the remaining juice from the pumpkin wedges. Cook the pumpkin for 5 min. After this, flip the pumpkin wedges into another side. Cook the pumpkin wedges for 3 min more. Then transfer the cooked pumpkin wedges into the serving plates. Sprinkle the pumpkin wedges with the raisins.

NUTRITION:

calories 119, fat 2.5, fiber 5.7, carbs 25.4, protein 2.1

CREAM CHEESE SPINACH

Prep time: 15 min | Cooking time: 10 min | Servings: 2

INGREDIENTS:

¼ cup cream	1 tsp butter
1 tbsp cream	½ tsp ground
cheese	black pepper
1 cup spinach	2 bacon slic-
½ onion, diced,	es, cooked,
boiled	chopped
½ tsp salt	½ tsp paprika

DIRECTIONS:

Preheat the air fryer to 330 F. Toss the butter in the air fryer basket and melt. Meanwhile, chop the spinach and sprinkle it with the salt. Let the spinach gives the juice. When the butter is melted – put the spinach with the remaining juice in the air fryer basket. Sprinkle the spinach with the cream cheese, cream, diced onion, ground black pepper, and paprika. Stir the mixture gently with the help of the wooden spatula. Cook the spinach for 5 min. After this, stir the spinach gently and add chopped bacon. Cook the spinach for 5 min more. Then stir the cooked meal carefully. Transfer the cooked spinach to the serving plates. Serve it!

NUTRITION:

calories 174, fat 13.4, fiber 1.3, carbs 5.1, protein 8.6

CREAMY LEEK

Prep time: 10 min | Cooking time: 11 min | Servings: 2

INGREDIENTS:

½ tsp baking	¼ tsp salt
soda	1 tbsp butter
1 tbsp sugar	3 tbsp chicken
11 oz leek	stock
3 tbsp cream	¼ tsp turmeric

DIRECTIONS:

Chop the leek. Preheat the air fryer to 390 F. Toss the butter there and melt it. Then add cream and chicken stock. After this, add the chopped leek. Sprinkle the leek with the sugar, salt, baking soda, and turmeric. Stir it carefully. Cook the leek for 5 min. After this, shake the leek carefully and cook for 6 min more. When the leek is soft and light brown – it is cooked. Let it chill for 3 min.

NUTRITION:

calories 182, fat 7.3, fiber 2.9, carbs 28.9, protein 2.6

PAPRIKA HASSELBACK POTATOES

Prep time: 15 min | Cooking time: 30 min | Servings: 2

INGREDIENTS:

2 medium potatoes
4 bacon slices
½ tsp salt
½ tsp ground black pepper
½ tsp ground paprika
1 tsp olive oil
½ tsp thyme
¼ tsp sage

DIRECTIONS:

Wash the potatoes carefully but do not peel them. Cut the slits in the potatoes to not cut them completely. Place the sliced bacon into the potato slits. Then sprinkle every Hasselback potato with the salt, ground black pepper, ground paprika, olive oil, thyme, and sage. Preheat the air fryer to 400 F. Put the Hasselback potatoes in the air fryer basket. Cook the Hasselback potatoes for 30 min. When the meal is cooked – chill it till the room temperature.

NUTRITION:

calories 376, fat 18.5, fiber 5.6, carbs 34.9, protein 17.8

MARINATED EGGPLANTS WITH SESAME SEEDS

Prep time: 20 min | Cooking time: 12 min | Servings: 2

INGREDIENTS:

2 eggplants
1 tbsp sesame seeds
1 tsp canola oil
1 tsp apple cider vinegar
½ tsp chili
flakes
¼ cup chicken stock
1 pinch salt
½ tsp lemon juice

DIRECTIONS:

Peel the eggplants and cut them into the medium cubes. Preheat the air fryer to 390 F. Put the eggplants in the air fryer basket and sprinkle with the chicken stock salt. Cook the eggplants for 8 min. Shake the eggplants after 4 min of cooking. Then drain the eggplants and transfer them to the bowl. Sprinkle the vegetables with the sesame seeds, apple cider vinegar, chili flakes, salt, and lemon juice. Mix the vegetables gently and put them in the fridge for at least 10 min to marinate. Serve the cooked meal cold.

NUTRITION:

calories 186, fat 5.6, fiber 19.9, carbs 33.4, protein 6.3

CHEDDAR MAC'N'CHEESE

Prep time: 15 min | Cooking time: 5 min | Servings: 2

INGREDIENTS:

6 oz mac, boiled
3 oz Cheddar cheese, shredded
2 oz Parmesan, shredded
1/3 cup half and half
1 tsp butter
½ tsp salt
½ tsp dried oregano

DIRECTIONS:

Toss the butter in the saucepan and melt it. Add half and half. Then sprinkle the liquid with the shredded Parmesan and Cheddar cheese. Add salt and dried oregano. Stir the mixture and simmer it on the medium heat for 3 min or till the cheese is melted and liquid is homogenous. Preheat the air fryer to 360 F. Put the cooked mac in the air fryer basket. Add the melted cheese mixture and stir. Cook the mac for 5 min. When the mac is cooked – it will have the light brown crust.

NUTRITION:

calories 578, fat 28.7, fiber 0.2, carbs 50.1, protein 30.6

WHITE OREGANO CABBAGE

Prep time: 10 min | Cooking time: 7 min | Servings: 2

INGREDIENTS:

12 oz white cabbage	½ tsp olive oil
1 tbsp onion powder	1 tsp oregano
1 tsp peanut butter	½ tbsp dried dill
	¼ tsp ground black pepper

DIRECTIONS:

Slice the cabbage into the thick wedges. Rub the cabbage with the onion powder, oregano, dried dill, and ground black pepper. Then sprinkle the cabbage wedges with the olive oil. Massage every cabbage wedge gently from each side. Preheat the air fryer to 360 F. Put the cabbage wedges in the air fryer basket. Add the peanut butter and cook the meal for 4 min. After this, flip the cabbage wedges to another side and cook for 3 min. Then transfer the cooked meal to the serving plates.

NUTRITION:

calories 85, fat 2.8, fiber 5.1, carbs 14.3, protein 3.5

CREAMY BROCCOLI FLORETS

Prep time: 15 min | Cooking time: 6 min | Servings: 2

INGREDIENTS:

1 egg	2 tbsp flour
¼ cup cream	1 tsp olive oil
½ tsp salt	12 oz broccoli

DIRECTIONS:

Wash the broccoli and separate it into the medium florets. Crack the egg into the bowl and whisk it. Combine the egg with the cream and salt. Stir the mixture. After this, dip the broccoli florets in the cream mixture. Then sprinkle every broccoli floret with the flour. Preheat the air fryer to 400 F. Put the broccoli florets in the air fryer tray. Cook the broccoli for 5 min. After this, shake the broccoli florets gently and cook them for 1 min. Then chill the broccoli gently and serve.

NUTRITION:

calories 157, fat 6.8, fiber 4.6, carbs 18.4, protein 8.6

DILL MASHED POTATO

Prep time: 10 min | Cooking time: 15 min | Servings: 2

INGREDIENTS:

2 potatoes	½ tsp salt
2 tbsp fresh dill, chopped	¼ cup half and half
1 tsp butter	

DIRECTIONS:

Preheat the air fryer to 390 F. Wash the potatoes carefully and place them in the air fryer. Cook the potatoes for 15 min. After this, remove the potatoes from the air fryer. Peel the potatoes. Mash the potatoes with the help of the fork well. Then add chopped fresh dill and salt. Stir it gently and add butter and half and half. Take the hand blender and blend the mixture well.

NUTRITION:

calories 211, fat 5.7, fiber 5.5, carbs 36.5, protein 5.1

BUTTERNUT SQUASH PUREE

Prep time: 10 min | Cooking time: 10 min | Servings: 2

INGREDIENTS:

½ tsp salt	¼ cup water
12 oz butternut squash	2 tbsp cream
	¼ tsp sage

½ tsp butter, unsalted

DIRECTIONS:
Chop the butternut squash and put it in the air fryer. Add water and shake it gently. Sprinkle the vegetables with the salt. Set the air fryer to 400 F. Cook the vegetables for 10 min. Meanwhile, melt the butter and combine it with the cream. Stir the mixture and add sage. When the butternut squash is cooked – blend it well with the help of the hand blender. Then add the cream mixture and stir it well with the help of the spoon. Serve the side dish hot.

NUTRITION:
calories 93, fat 1.8, fiber 3.4, carbs 20.3, protein 1.8

CREAM POTATO
Prep time: 15 min | Cooking time: 20 min | Servings: 2

INGREDIENTS:

3 medium potatoes, scrubbed	1 tbsp Italian seasoning
½ tsp kosher salt	1/3 cup cream
	½ tsp ground black pepper

DIRECTIONS:
Slice the potatoes. Preheat the air fryer to 365 F. Make the layer from the sliced potato in the air fryer basket. Sprinkle the potato layer with the kosher salt and ground black pepper. After this, make the second layer of the potato and sprinkle it with Italian seasoning. Make the last layer of the sliced potato and pour the cream. Cook the scallop potato for 20 min.

NUTRITION:
calories 269, fat 4.7, fiber 7.8, carbs 52.6, protein 5.8

TOMATO NUTMEG ZUCCHINI
Prep time: 10 min | Cooking time: 8 min | Servings: 2

INGREDIENTS:

1 zucchini	½ tsp ground black pepper
½ onion, diced	½ tsp salt
2 tbsp tomato sauce	1 pinch ground nutmeg
1 tsp olive oil	

DIRECTIONS:
Wash the zucchini and grate it with the help of the grater. After this, combine together the grated zucchini and diced onion. Place the mixture in the air fryer tray. Sprinkle it with the olive oil, ground black pepper, salt, and nutmeg. Stir the zucchini mixture gently with the help of the wooden spatula. Preheat the air fryer to 390 F. Cook the zucchini mixture for 5 min. After this, stir the zucchini mixture carefully and add the tomato sauce. Mix it up and cook for 3 min more at 400 F. When the meal is cooked – stir it gently one more time and chill to the room temperature.

NUTRITION:
calories 52, fat 2.6, fiber 2.1, carbs 7.1, protein 1.8

CABBAGE WITH TOMATO
Prep time: 20 min | Cooking time: 10 min | Servings: 2

INGREDIENTS:

1 tsp sugar	½ tsp turmeric
14 oz cabbage	2 tbsp fresh parsley, chopped
1 yellow onion	
½ carrot, grated	1 tbsp olive oil
4 tbsp chicken stock	¼ cup tomato sauce
¼ tsp sriracha	1 garlic clove, sliced
1 tbsp dried cilantro	
1/3 tsp salt	

Shred the cabbage and toss it in the bowl. Sprinkle the shredded cabbage with the salt and turmeric. Mix it up with the help of the hands and leave for 5 min. Meanwhile, preheat the air fryer to 390 F. Sprinkle the air fryer basket with the olive oil and place the cabbage there. Sprinkle the cabbage with the grated carrot, chicken stock, sriracha, dried cilantro, turmeric, olive oil, and sliced garlic. After this, add the tomato sauce and stir the cabbage carefully. Cook it for 2 min. Meanwhile, peel the yellow onion and dice it. When the time is over – add the diced yellow onion in the air fryer basket, Add sugar and fresh parsley. Stir the cabbage mixture carefully until homogenous. Increase the temperature to 400 F and cook the meal for 5 min more. After this, stir the cabbage meal carefully with the help of the wooden spatula and cook for 3 min more.

NUTRITION:
calories 160, fat 7.5, fiber 7.3, carbs 23.1, protein 4

OREGANO GARLIC HEADS
Prep time: 10 min | Cooking time: 10 min | Servings: 2

INGREDIENTS:

2 garlic heads, (10 cloves)
1 tsp dried oregano
½ tsp dried parsley
2 tbsp olive oil
¼ tsp ground black pepper
¼ tsp ground thyme
¼ tsp ground nutmeg

DIRECTIONS:
Preheat the air fryer to 390 F. Combine the dried oregano, dried parsley, ground black pepper, ground thyme, and ground nutmeg in the shallow bowl. Shake the bowl gently to make the spice mixture homogenous. After this, cut the ends of the garlic heads. Rub the garlic heads with the spicy mixture. Then sprinkle every garlic head with 1 tbsp of olive oil. Wrap the garlic heads in the foil and place them in the air fryer basket. Cook the garlic heads for 10 min. After this, let the cooked garlic heads chill gently.

NUTRITION:
calories 192, fat 14.4, fiber 1.5, carbs 15.8, protein 3

FETA BEET CUBES
Prep time: 10 min | Cooking time: 12 min | Servings: 2

INGREDIENTS:

2 small beets
½ tsp salt
3 oz Feta cheese
1 tbsp olive oil
½ tsp sesame oil
¼ tsp dried oregano
1/3 tsp dried thyme
1 tsp fresh celery, chopped

DIRECTIONS:
Peel the beets and cut into the medium cubes. Put the beet cubes in the bowl and sprinkle with salt, dried oregano, and dried thyme. Shake the beets gently. Preheat the air fryer to 365 F. Sprinkle the beet cubes with the olive oil and shake well. After this, put the beet cubes in the air fryer basket and cook for 12 min or until the beets are tender.Transfer the cooked beets to the serving bowl. Add the chopped fresh celery and sesame oil. Then scramble Feta cheese over the beets.

NUTRITION:
calories 227, fat 17.4, fiber 2.2, carbs 12, protein 7.8

EGGPLANT & ZUCCHINI MIX

Prep time: 15 min | Cooking time: 14 min | Servings: 2

INGREDIENTS:

1 eggplant	black pepper
1 zucchini	1 tsp salt
1 red sweet	1 tbsp fresh
pepper	lemon juice
2 oz green	1 tsp butter
beans	½ white onion,
½ apple	sliced
1 tomato	1 tbsp tomato
1 tbsp Italian	sauce
seasoning	1 garlic clove,
2 tbsp olive oil	peeled
½ tsp ground	¼ tsp sage

DIRECTIONS:

Peel the eggplants and chop it. Chop the zucchini into the same pieces as the eggplant. After this, discard the seeds from the sweet pepper and chop it. Place all the vegetables in the mixing bowl. Add green beans. Chop the apple and add it to the mixture too. After this, chop the tomato and add it to the vegetable mixture. Sprinkle the vegetables with the olive oil, Italian seasoning, ground black pepper, salt, fresh lemon juice, sliced onion, tomato sauce, and sage. Slice the garlic clove and sprinkle over the vegetable mixture. Then toss the butter in the air fryer and preheat it to 370 F. When the butter is melted – transfer the vegetable mixture to the air fryer basket. Cook the vegetables for 7 min. After this, shake the vegetables carefully. Cook the meal for 7 min more. When all the vegetables are tender – the meal is cooked. Shake it one more time and transfer to the serving plates.

NUTRITION:

calories 312, fat 19.1, fiber 13.6, carbs 37, protein 5.7

CHARD WITH CHEDDAR

Prep time: 10 min | Cooking time: 11 min | Servings: 2

INGREDIENTS:

3 oz Cheddar	1 tbsp sesame
cheese, grated	oil
10 oz Swiss	½ tsp salt
chard	½ tsp ground
3 tbsp cream	white pepper

DIRECTIONS:

Wash Swiss chard carefully and chop it roughly. After this, sprinkle chopped Swiss chard with the salt and ground white pepper. Stir it carefully. Sprinkle Swiss chard with the sesame oil and stir it carefully with the help of 2 spatulas. Preheat the air fryer to 260 F. Put chopped Swiss chard in the air fryer basket and cook for 6 min. Shake it after 3 min of cooking. Then pour the cream into the air fryer basket and mix it up. Cook the meal for 3 min more. Then increase the temperature to 400 F. Sprinkle the meal with the grated cheese and cook for 2 min more. After this, transfer the meal in the serving plates.

NUTRITION:

calories 272, fat 22.3, fiber 2.5, carbs 6.7, protein 13.3

SWEET POTATO CUBES

Prep time: 10 min | Cooking time: 13 min | Servings: 2

INGREDIENTS:

2 sweet pota-	¼ tsp chili
toes (yum)	flakes
1 tbsp olive oil	1/3 tsp salt
½ tsp ground	½ tsp butter
thyme	

DIRECTIONS:

Peel the sweet potatoes and cut them into the medium cubes.

Then combine together the chili flakes, salt, and ground thyme. Melt the butter and combine it with the olive oil. Add the spice mixture and churn it. Sprinkle the sweet potato cubes with the churned olive oil mixture. Shake it well. Preheat the air fryer to 360 F. Put the sweet potato cubes in the air fryer basket and cook for 10 min. Shake the meal well and cook for 3 min more. When the sweet potato is tender – it is cooked. Let it chill gently. Serve it!

NUTRITION:
calories 70, fat 8, fiber 0.1, carbs 0.5, protein 0.1

SWEET ONION RINGS
Prep time: 10 min | Cooking time: 5 min | Servings: 2

INGREDIENTS:

2 white onions	¼ tsp turmeric
1 tbsp brown sugar	1 tsp olive oil
1 pinch salt	1 tbsp corn-starch

DIRECTIONS:
Peel the onions and cut them into the thick rings. Then combine together the brown sugar and salt. Add turmeric and cornstarch. Mix it up. Put the onion rings in a bowl and sprinkle them generously with the brown sugar mixture. Preheat the air fryer to 400 F. Put the onion rings in the air fryer basket and sprinkle with the olive oil. Shake them gently and cook for 5 min. Shake the onion rings after 3 min of cooking. The cooked onion rings should not be crunchy. Serve the meal immediately.

NUTRITION:
calories 77, fat 0.1, fiber 2.5, carbs 18.5, protein 1.3

OLIVE OIL OKRA
Prep time: 10 min | Cooking time: 7 min | Servings: 2

INGREDIENTS:

1 tsp garlic powder	½ tsp salt
4 garlic cloves	1 egg
10 oz okra	¼ tsp ground black pepper
1 tsp olive oil	

DIRECTIONS:
Crack the egg into the bowl and whisk it. Sprinkle the whisked egg with the salt and ground black pepper. Then add the garlic powder and stir it carefully. Mince the garlic cloves and add them to the egg mixture. Stir it gently. Put the okra in the egg mixture and mix up it. Preheat the air fryer to 400 F. Put the okra in the air fryer basket and cook it for 7 min. Shake okra after 5 min of cooking. Then let the cooked meal chill little. Serve it!

NUTRITION:
calories 122, fat 4.8, fiber 4.9, carbs 13.9, protein 6.2

MUSHROOMS & CREAM
Prep time: 10 min | Cooking time: 8 min | Servings: 2

INGREDIENTS:

9 oz mushrooms	¼ tsp salt
3 tbsp cream	½ onion, grated
1 tsp flour	1 tbsp butter
¼ tsp ground black pepper	¼ green chili, chopped

DIRECTIONS:
Wash the mushrooms and slice them. Sprinkle the mushrooms with ground black pepper and salt. Stir the mixture. Preheat the air fryer to 360 F. Toss the butter in the air fryer basket and melt it. When the butter is melted – add

the sliced mushrooms in the air fryer. Stir the mushrooms and cook them for 5 min. Meanwhile, combine together flour, cream, and grated onion. Add chili pepper and whisk it until homogenous. Then pour the cream mixture over the mushrooms and stir it. Increase the temperature to 400 F and cook the meal for 3 min more.

NUTRITION:
calories 106, fat 7.2, fiber 2, carbs 8.5, protein 4.7

MEXICAN PARMESAN CORN
Prep time: 5 min | Cooking time: 13 min | Servings: 2

INGREDIENTS:

1 tbsp green chili powder
2 tbsp mayonnaise
2 corn on cobs
3 oz Parmesan, shredded
½ tsp salt
1/3 tsp olive oil

DIRECTIONS:
Preheat the air fryer to 365 F. Sprinkle the corn with the salt and olive oil. Put the rack in the air fryer. Place the corn on the cobs on the rack and cook it for 13 min. Then remove the corn from the cobs from the air fryer and brush it with the mayonnaise from all sides. Combine together the green chili powder and shredded Parmesan. Then sprinkle the corn with the cheese mixture.

NUTRITION:
calories 213, fat 15.4, fiber 1.3, carbs 7.3, protein 14.3

TAHINI EGGPLANTS
Prep time: 20 min | Cooking time: 15 min | Servings: 2

INGREDIENTS:

1 tsp tahini
2 tbsp soy sauce
3 tbsp fresh lemon juice
½ tsp sesame seeds
¼ tsp salt
½ tsp brown sugar
1 tbsp olive oil
2 eggplants
1 garlic clove, chopped
½ tsp garlic powder

DIRECTIONS:
Peel the eggplants and chop them roughly. Combine together the soy sauce and fresh lemon juice. Sprinkle the chopped eggplants with the soy-lemon mixture. Then sprinkle the vegetables with the salt, brown sugar, chopped garlic clove, and garlic powder. Add tahini and mix it up. Leave the eggplants mixture for 15 min in the fridge. Preheat the air fryer to 400 F. Put the eggplants and remaining liquid from the eggplants in the air fryer basket. Cook the vegetables for 15 min. Shake the eggplants every 4 min. When the eggplants cooked – shake them one more time and sprinkle with the sesame seeds and olive oil. Stir the eggplants and serve.

NUTRITION:
calories 238, fat 9.9, fiber 20, carbs 36.4, protein 7.3

CREAM CHEESE CAULIFLOWER
Prep time: 10 min | Cooking time: 12 min | Servings: 2

INGREDIENTS:

1 tsp tahini
1/3 cup cream
13 oz cauliflower
½ onion, diced, sautéed
½ tsp salt
½ tsp garlic powder
1 tsp cream cheese
½ tsp butter

DIRECTIONS:
Wash the cauliflower carefully and chop it. Sprinkle the

chopped cauliflower with the salt and garlic powder. Shake the mixture. Preheat the air fryer to 400 F. Put the cauliflower in the air fryer basket. Add cream and cream cheese. After this, add butter and shake the mixture gently. Cook the cauliflower for 12 min. Shake the cauliflower after 6 min of cooking. Then transfer the cooked cauliflower to the mixing bowl. Blend it well with the help of the hand blender. When the mixture is smooth – add sautéed onion and mix up it. Serve the meal warm.

NUTRITION:
calories 114, fat 5.3, fiber 5.5, carbs 14.7, protein 5

FETA CHEESE POTATO SLICES
Prep time: 10 min | Cooking time: 14 min | Servings: 2

INGREDIENTS:

1 egg	1 tbsp butter
3 oz Feta cheese, scrambled	¼ tsp paprika
	½ tsp ground black pepper
4 potatoes	½ tsp turmeric
½ tsp salt	2 tbsp cream

DIRECTIONS:
Peel the potatoes and slice them. Sprinkle the sliced potatoes with the salt, paprika, ground black pepper, and turmeric. Mix the potatoes. Preheat the air fryer to 390 F. Toss the butter in the air fryer basket and melt it. Then place the potato slices in the air fryer basket. Beat the egg and whisk it. Pour the whisked egg over the potatoes. Add cream and cook the potatoes for 10 min. Then sprinkle the potatoes with Feta cheese and cook potato for 4 min more. When the meal is cooked – let it chill till the room temperature and serve.

52

NUTRITION:
calories 500, fat 18.2, fiber 10.6, carbs 70, protein 16.3

THYME FENNEL
Prep time: 10 min | Cooking time: 10 min | Servings: 2

INGREDIENTS:

1 tbsp thyme	1 pinch salt
12 oz fennel	1 pinch ground black pepper
1 tbsp brown sugar	½ tsp chili flakes
1 tbsp butter	
½ tsp olive oil	

DIRECTIONS:
Preheat the air fryer to 365 F. Chop the fennel roughly. Sprinkle the fennel with the salt, ground black pepper, and chili flakes. Mix the mixture. Sprinkle the fennel with the olive oil and place in the air fryer. Cook the fennel for 8 min. Flip the fennel after 4 min of the cooking. Meanwhile, melt the butter and combine it together with the thyme and brown sugar. Whisk the mixture until the sugar is dissolved. Then sprinkle the fennel with the sugar mixture and cook for 2 min more. Serve the cooked meal immediately.

NUTRITION:
calories 135, fat 7.4, fiber 5.8, carbs 17.7, protein 2.3

CHILI SQUASH WEDGES
Prep time: 10 min | Cooking time: 18 min | Servings: 2

INGREDIENTS:

11 oz Acorn squash	½ tsp chili pepper
½ tsp salt	½ tsp paprika
1 tbsp olive oil	

DIRECTIONS:

Cut Acorn squash into the serving wedges. Sprinkle the wedges with the salt, olive oil, chili pepper, and paprika. Massage the wedges gently. Preheat the air fryer to 400 F. Put Acorn squash wedges in the air fryer basket and cook for 18 min. Flip the wedges into another side after 9 min of cooking. Serve the cooked meal hot.

NUTRITION:

calories 125, fat 7.2, fiber 2.6, carbs 16.7, protein 1.4

PAPRIKA YELLOW SQUASH

Prep time: 10 min | Cooking time: 12 min | Servings: 2

INGREDIENTS:

10 oz yellow squash	½ tsp ground black pepper
1 yellow onion	1 tbsp mayonnaise
¼ cup chicken stock	3 tsp lemon juice
1 tbsp olive oil	2 oz Cheddar, shredded
¼ tsp paprika	
¼ tsp salt	

DIRECTIONS:

Chop the yellow squash and put it in the bowl. Sprinkle the yellow squash with the chicken stock, olive oil, paprika, salt, and ground black pepper. Shake the vegetables carefully. Then preheat the air fryer to 390 F. Put the yellow squash in the air fryer basket and cook for 7 min. After this, shake the yellow squash. Combine together the mayonnaise with fresh lemon juice and shredded cheese. Put the mayonnaise mixture in the air fryer and mix it up. Cook the meal at 400 F for 4 min more.

NUTRITION:

calories 188, fat 11.9, fiber 3, carbs 12.9, protein 9.6

PUFF CAULIFLOWER PATTIES

Prep time: 10 min | Cooking time: 9 min | Servings: 2

INGREDIENTS:

3 oz puff pastry	½ tsp cumin
7 oz mashed cauliflower	¼ tsp salt
1 egg yolk	1 oz carrot, sautéed

DIRECTIONS:

Roll the puff pastry and cut it into the triangles. Then combine the sautéed carrot with the mashed cauliflower. Place the filing on the triangles and secure them well. Whisk the egg and brush the patties. Sprinkle the patties with the cumin and salt. Preheat the air fryer to 390 F. Put the patties on the air fryer rack and cook for 9 min. When the patties are golden brown – they are cooked. Transfer them to the serving plates.

NUTRITION:

calories 333, fat 24.4, fiber 2.8, carbs 23.4, protein 6.4

COTTAGE CHEESE MUSHROOMS

Prep time: 10 min | Cooking time: 6 min | Servings: 2

INGREDIENTS:

3 oz Parmesan, shredded	¼ tsp minced garlic
3 oz cottage cheese	½ tsp butter
2 tbsp fresh parsley, chopped	2 Portobello mushroom hats
	1/3 tsp salt

DIRECTIONS:

Peel the mushroom hats. Combine together chopped parsley, minced garlic, cottage cheese, salt, and butter. Mix it with the help of the hand blender. Preheat the air fryer to 400 F. Fill the mushrooms with the cottage cheese mixture and put them in the air fryer basket. Cook the mushrooms for 4 min. Then sprinkle the mushrooms with the shredded cheese and cook for 2 min more. Let the cooked mushrooms chill gently. Serve the meal!

NUTRITION:
calories 205, fat 10.9, fiber 1.1, carbs 6.4, protein 22.7

HONEY CARROTS WITH GREENS
Prep time: 7 min | Cooking time: 12 min | Servings: 2

INGREDIENTS:

1 cup baby carrot	pepper
½ tsp salt	1 tbsp honey
½ tsp white	1 tsp sesame oil

DIRECTIONS:
Preheat the air fryer to 385 F. Combine the baby carrot with the salt, white pepper, and sesame oil. Shake the baby carrot and transfer in the air fryer basket. Cook the vegetables for 10 min. After this, add honey and shake the vegetables. Cook the meal for 2 min. After this, shake the vegetables and serve immediately.

NUTRITION:
calories 83, fat 2.4, fiber 2.6, carbs 16, protein 0.6

CREAMY RED POTATOES
Prep time: 15 min | Cooking time: 10 min | Servings: 2

INGREDIENTS:

4 red potatoes	cheese
¼ cup cream	½ tbsp onion

powder
4 tbsp chicken stock

½ tsp salt
1 tbsp butter
½ tsp olive oil

DIRECTIONS:
Wash the potatoes and peel them. Chop the potatoes roughly and sprinkle with the olive oil and salt. Preheat the air fryer to 400 F. Put the potato in the air fryer basket and add butter. Cook the potato for 10 min. Shake the potato after 7 min of cooking. After this, smash the potatoes with the help of the fork. Add onion powder, chicken stock, and cream cheese. Mix the potatoes until homogenous and serve. Taste it!

NUTRITION:
calories 468, fat 17.7, fiber 7.3, carbs 70, protein 10.6

SNACKS AND APPETIZERS
Sesame Tofu Cubes
Prep time: 20 min | Cooking time: 20 min | Servings: 2

INGREDIENTS:

8 oz tofu	1 tsp rice vinegar
1 tsp cornstarch	
1 tsp scallions, chopped	1 tsp sesame oil
	1 tsp soy sauce

DIRECTIONS:
Cut the tofu into the cubes. Put the tofu cubes in the bowl and sprinkle with the rice vinegar, sesame oil, and soy sauce. Shake the mixture. Leave the tofu for 10 min to marinate. Preheat the air fryer to 370 F. Sprinkle the marinated tofu with the cornstarch and put in the air fryer basket. Cook tofu for 20 min. Shake the tofu after 11 min of cooking. Then chill the tofu gently and sprinkle with the chopped scallions.

NUTRITION:
calories 108, fat 7, fiber 1.1, carbs 3.4, protein 9.5

THYME SALTY TOMATOES
Prep time: 10 min | Cooking time: 10 min | Servings: 2

INGREDIENTS:

2 tomatoes   1 pinch salt
1 tbsp thyme   1 tsp olive oil

DIRECTIONS:
Preheat the air fryer to 375 F. Slice the tomatoes. Then combine together thyme and salt. Shake the mixture. Sprinkle the sliced tomatoes with the thyme mixture. Place the sliced tomatoes in the air fryer and spray with the olive oil. Cook the tomatoes for 10 min. When the tomatoes are cooked – they should have tender and little bit dry texture.

NUTRITION:
calories 46, fat 2.7, fiber 2, carbs 5.6, protein 1.2

CREAMY CHICKEN LIVER
Prep time: 10 min | Cooking time: 10 min | Servings: 2

INGREDIENTS:

7 oz chicken   2 tsp cream
liver   1 tbsp fresh
¼ cup water   dill, chopped
1 tbsp butter   1 pinch salt

DIRECTIONS:
Preheat the air fryer to 390 F. Combine together water, chicken liver, and salt. Mix the mixture and place it in the air fryer basket. Cook the chicken liver for 10 min. Stir it after 5 min of cooking. Then transfer the cooked chicken liver to the bowl. Add cream and butter. Blend the mixture until smooth. After this, add chopped fresh dill and stir gently.

NUTRITION:
calories 223, fat 12.5, fiber 0.2, carbs 1.9, protein 24.7

CATFISH STICKS
Prep time: 10 min | Cooking time: 10 min | Servings: 2

INGREDIENTS:

8 oz catfish   ¼ cup panko
fillet   breadcrumbs
½ tsp salt   1 egg
½ tsp ground   ½ tsp olive oil
black pepper

DIRECTIONS:
Cut the catfish fillet into 2 medium pieces (sticks). Then sprinkle the catfish with the salt and ground black pepper. Beat the egg in the bowl and whisk it. Dip the catfish fillets in the whisked egg. After this, coat the fish in the panko breadcrumbs. Preheat the air fryer to 380 F. Put the fish sticks in the air fryer basket and spray with the olive oil. Cook the fish sticks for 10 min. Flip the sticks into another side after 10 min of cooking. When the fish sticks are cooked – let them chill gently. Serve the meal!

NUTRITION:
calories 231, fat 12.2, fiber 1.1, carbs 8, protein 21.5

HONEY BANANA CHIPS
Prep time: 10 min | Cooking time: 6 min | Servings: 2

INGREDIENTS:

2 bananas   pepper
1 tsp honey   ½ tsp olive oil
1 pinch white

DIRECTIONS:
Peel the bananas and slice them into the chips pieces. Then sprinkle the bananas with the honey and white pepper. Spray the olive oil over the bananas and mix them gently with the help of the hands. Preheat the air fryer to 320 F. Put the banana chips in the air

fryer basket and cook for 6 min.

NUTRITION:
calories 126, fat 1.6, fiber 3.1, carbs 29.9, protein 1.3

GINGER APPLE CHIPS
Prep time: 8 min | Cooking time: 10 min | Servings: 2

INGREDIENTS:

½ tsp olive oil
3 apples

1 pinch ground ginger

DIRECTIONS:
Peel the apples and remove the seeds. Slice the apples and sprinkle them with the ground ginger and olive oil. Preheat the air fryer to 400 F. Place the apple slices on the air fryer rack. Cook the apple chips for 10 min. Shake the apple chips carefully after 4 min of cooking. Then chill the apple chips carefully. Serve the meal immediately or keep it in the paper bag in the dry place.

NUTRITION:
calories 184, fat 1.8, fiber 8.1, carbs 46.3, protein 0.9

MAPLE CARROT FRIES
Prep time: 5 min | Cooking time: 10 min | Servings: 2

INGREDIENTS:

1 cup baby carrot
¼ cup maple syrup
1 pinch salt
½ tsp thyme

½ tsp ground black pepper
1 tsp dried oregano
1 tbsp olive oil

DIRECTIONS:
Preheat the air fryer to 410 F. Place the baby carrot in the air fryer basket. Sprinkle the baby carrot with the thyme, salt, ground black pepper, and dried oregano. Then spray the olive oil

over the baby carrot and shake it well. Cook the baby carrot fries for 10 min. Shake the carrot fries after 6 min of cooking. Chill the cooked meal for 5 min.

NUTRITION:
calories 197, fat 7.3, fiber 3, carbs 34.4, protein 0.7

SWEET POTATO FRIES
Prep time: 10 min | Cooking time: 15 min | Servings: 2

INGREDIENTS:

2 sweet potatoes
1 tbsp coconut oil
1/3 tsp salt

½ tsp ground black pepper
½ tsp onion powder

DIRECTIONS:
Preheat the air fryer to 370 F. Peel the sweet potatoes and cut them into the fries. Sprinkle the vegetables with the salt, ground black pepper, and onion powder. Shake the sweet potatoes and sprinkle with the coconut oil. Put the uncooked sweet potato fries in the air fryer basket and cook for 15 min. Shake the sweet potato fries every 5 min. When the sweet potato fries are cooked – let them chill gently.

NUTRITION:
calories 225, fat 6.8, fiber 5.2, carbs 42.1, protein 2.6

SQUID RINGS
Prep time: 10 min | Cooking time: 4 min | Servings: 2

INGREDIENTS:

2 squid tubes
2 eggs
1/3 cup flour
¼ tsp salt

½ tsp onion powder
½ tsp garlic powder

DIRECTIONS:
Wash and peel the squid cubes carefully. Then slice the squid cubes into the rings. Beat the eggs in the bowl and whisk them. Then dip the squid rings in the whisked eggs. Combine together flour, salt, onion powder, and garlic powder. Stir the mixture with the help of the fork. Then coat the squid rings with the flour mixture. Preheat the air fryer to 400 F. Put the squid rings onto the air fryer rack. Cook the squid rings for 4 min. Shake the squid rings after 3 min of cooking. When the squid rings are cooked – let them chill till the room temperature.

NUTRITION:
calories 383, fat 10.5, fiber 0.7, carbs 17.2, protein 55.8

CARROT CHIPS
Prep time: 10 min | Cooking time: 20 min | Servings: 2

INGREDIENTS:

3 carrots	black pepper
½ tsp salt	1 tbsp canola
½ tsp ground	oil

DIRECTIONS:
Peel the carrot and slice into the chips. Then sprinkle the un-cooked carrot chips with the salt, ground black pepper, and canola oil. Shake the carrot chips carefully. Preheat the air fryer to 360 F. Put the carrot chips in the air fryer basket. Shake the carrot chips in halfway. Check the doneness of the carrot chips while cooking. Chill the carrot chips and serve.

NUTRITION:
calories 101, fat 7, fiber 2.4, carbs 9.3, protein 0.8

CORN OKRA BITES
Prep time: 10 min | Cooking time: 4 min | Servings: 2

INGREDIENTS:

4 tbsp corn	1 egg
flakes, crushed	½ tsp salt
9 oz okra	1 tsp olive oil

DIRECTIONS:
Preheat the air fryer to 400 F. Chop the okra roughly. Combine together the corn flakes and salt. Crack the egg into the bowl and whisk it. Toss the chopped okra in the whisked egg. Then coat the chopped okra with the corn flakes. Put the chopped okra in the air fryer basket and sprinkle with the olive oil. Cook the okra for 4 min. Shake the okra after 2 min of cooking. When the okra is cooked – let it chill gently.

NUTRITION:
calories 115, fat 4.8, fiber 4.2, carbs 12.7, protein 5.2

SALTY POTATO CHIPS
Prep time: 10 min | Cooking time: 19 min | Servings: 2

INGREDIENTS:

3 potatoes	oil
1 tbsp canola	½ tsp salt

DIRECTIONS:
Wash the potatoes carefully and do not peel them. Slice the potatoes into the chips. Sprinkle the potato chips with the olive oil and salt. Mix the potatoes carefully. Preheat the air fryer to 400 F. Put the potato chips in the air fryer basket and cook for 19 min. Shake the potato chips every 3 min.

NUTRITION:
calories 282, fat 7.3, fiber 7.7, carbs 50.2, protein 5.4

CORN & BEANS FRIES
Prep time: 10 min | Cooking time: 7 min | Servings: 2

INGREDIENTS:

¼ cup corn flakes crumbs	1 tbsp canola oil
1 egg	½ tsp salt
10 oz green beans	1 tsp garlic powder

DIRECTIONS:
Preheat the air fryer to 400 F. Put the green beans in the bowl. Beat the egg in the green beans and stir carefully until homogenous. Then sprinkle the green beans with the salt and garlic powder. Shake gently. Then coat the green beans in the corn flakes crumbs well. Put the green beans in the air fryer basket in one layer. Cook the green beans for 7 min. Shake the green beans twice during the cooking. When the green beans are cooked – let them chill and serve.

NUTRITION:
calories 182, fat 9.4, fiber 5.3, carbs 21, protein 6.3

SUGARY APPLE FRITTERS
Prep time: 10 min | Cooking time: 8 min | Servings: 2

INGREDIENTS:

2 red apples	juice
1 tsp sugar	½ tsp ground cinnamon
1 tbsp flour	
1 tbsp semolina	1 tsp butter
1 tsp lemon	1 egg

DIRECTIONS:
Peel the apples and grate them. Sprinkle the grated apples with the lemon juice. Then add sugar, flour, semolina, and ground cinnamon. Mix the mixture and crack the egg. Mix the apple mixture carefully. Preheat the air fryer to 370 F. Toss the butter in the air fryer basket and melt it. When the butter is melted – make the medium fritters from the apple mixture. Use 2 spoons for this step. Place the fritters in the air fryer basket and cook for 6 min. After this, flip the fritters to another side and cook for 2 min more. Dry the cooked fritters with the help of the paper towel and serve.

NUTRITION:
calories 207, fat 4.6, fiber 6, carbs 40.3, protein 4.5

CHILI ONION RINGS
Prep time: 15 min | Cooking time: min | Servings: 2

INGREDIENTS:

1 tbsp oregano	½ tsp salt
1 tbsp flour	2 white onions, peeled
½ tsp corn-starch	
1 egg	1 tbsp olive oil

DIRECTIONS:
Crack the egg into the bowl and whisk it. Combine together the flour and cornstarch in the separate bowl. Add oregano and salt. Shake the mixture gently. Peel the onions and slice them to get the "rings". Then dip the onion rings in the whisked egg. After this, coat the onion rings in the flour mixture. Preheat the air fryer to 365 F. Spray the air fryer basket with the olive oil inside. Then place the onion rings in the air fryer and cook for 8 min. Shake the onion rings after 4 min of cooking. Let the cooked meal chill gently. Serve it!

NUTRITION:
calories 159, fat 9.6, fiber 3.4, carbs 15.5, protein 4.6

PEPPER GREEN TOMATOES

Prep time: 10 min | Cooking time: 18 min | Servings: 2

INGREDIENTS:

4 green tomatoes	1/3 tsp salt
1 egg	½ tsp ground black pepper
¼ cup flour	¼ tbsp olive oil

DIRECTIONS:

Wash the green tomatoes and slice them. Beat the egg in the bowl and whisk it. Combine together the whisked egg and flour. Add salt and ground black pepper. Stir the mixture well. After this, dip the tomato slices in the whisked egg mixture. Preheat the air fryer to 360 F. Put the green tomatoes on air fryer rack and cook for 18 min. Flip the tomatoes in the halfway mark. Let the cooked meal chill till the room temperature.

NUTRITION:

calories 149, fat 4.6, fiber 3.5, carbs 22, protein 6.6

AVOCADO SUSHI

Prep time: 15 min | Cooking time: 4 min | Servings: 2

INGREDIENTS:

1 sheet sushi nori	5 oz sushi salmon
½ tsp garlic powder	5 oz sushi rice, cooked
2 tsp soy sauce	2 oz avocado
¼ tsp rice vinegar	¼ cup panko breadcrumbs
1 tsp sesame seeds, roasted	1 tbsp mayo sauce

DIRECTIONS:

Combine the sushi rice with the soy sauce and rice vinegar. Stir the mixture. Then spread the sushi nori with the rice. After this, cut the avocado into the strips. Put the avocado strips in the center of the sushi nori. Then add salmon. Sprinkle the salmon with the garlic powder and sesame seeds. Roll the sushi nori to make the shape of a stick. After this, spread the sushi stick with the mayo sauce well. Preheat the air fryer to 400 F. Coat the sushi stick in the panko breadcrumbs and place in the air fryer rack. Cook the sushi for 4 min. Flip the sushi stick after 2 min of cooking. Then slice sushi into 6 pieces.

NUTRITION:

calories 453, fat 9.5, fiber 4.6, carbs 67.9, protein 21.9

MAYO CAULIFLOWER FLORETS

Prep time: 15 min | Cooking time: 12 min | Servings: 2

INGREDIENTS:

1 tbsp Buffalo sauce	9 oz cauliflower florets
1 tbsp mayo sauce	¼ cup panko breadcrumbs, Italian seasoned
1 tbsp butter, melted	
1 pinch salt	

DIRECTIONS:

Combine together the melted butter, Buffalo sauce, and mayo sauce. Whisk the mixture well. Add salt and stir it gently. Then coat the cauliflower florets in Buffalo sauce mixture well. Preheat the air fryer to 360 F. Transfer Buffalo cauliflower in the air fryer basket and cook for 12 min, Shake the cauliflower after 7 min of cooking. When the meal is cooked – chill it for 2-3 min and serve.

NUTRITION:

calories 189, fat 13, fiber 3.9, carbs 16.3, protein 4.1

SMOKED CASHEWS
Prep time: 8 min | Cooking time: 8 min | Servings: 2

INGREDIENTS:

1 tsp liquid smoke	shews
8 oz raw ca-	¼ tsp salt
	¼ tsp sugar

DIRECTIONS:
Put the raw cashews in the bowl. Add liquid smoke, salt, and sugar. Shake the mixture well. After this, preheat the air fryer to 350 F. Put the cashews in the air fryer basket and cook for 8 min. Shake the cashews every 2 min of cooking. Cook the cashews 1 extra min if desired. Then chill the cashews to the room temperature.

NUTRITION:
calories 653, fat 52.6, fiber 3.4, carbs 37.6, protein 17.4

TOASTED SALTY WALNUTS
Prep time: 5 min | Cooking time: 5 min | Servings: 2

INGREDIENTS:

1 tsp salt	flakes
5 oz walnuts	½ tsp ground
¼ tsp chili	nutmeg

DIRECTIONS:
Preheat the air fryer to 350 F. Put the walnuts in the air fryer basket. Sprinkle the walnuts with the chili flakes and salt. Add ground nutmeg and shake the walnuts. Cook the walnuts for 3 min. After this, increase the temperature to 360 F. Shake the walnuts carefully and cook for 2 min more. Then shake the walnuts and chill them.

NUTRITION:
calories 441, fat 42, fiber 4.9, carbs 7.3, protein 17.1

CINNAMON DOUGH BITES
Prep time: 10 min | Cooking time: 6 min | Servings: 2

INGREDIENTS:

4 tbsp flour	1 tsp ground cinnamon
½ tsp baking powder	1 egg
½ tsp apple cider vinegar	1 tbsp margarine
1 tbsp brown sugar	¼ tsp nutmeg

DIRECTIONS:
Beat the egg in the bowl and whisk it. Melt the margarine and combine it together with the whisked egg. Add nutmeg, apple cider vinegar, brown sugar, baking powder, and flour. Knead the smooth and non-sticky dough. Then make 4 bites from the dough. Preheat the air fryer to 400 F. Place the sweet bites on the air fryer rack and cook for 4 min. Then flip the bites to another side and cook for 2 min more.

NUTRITION:
calories 162, fat 8.1, fiber 1.1, carbs 18.2, protein 4.5

SALTY GARLIC PRETZELS
Prep time: 20 min | Cooking time: 4 min | Servings: 2

INGREDIENTS:

3 tbsp boiling water	1 pinch salt
7 tbsp flour	½ tbsp garlic powder
1 pinch dry yeast	1 tsp olive oil
	½ tsp sugar

DIRECTIONS:
Combine together the dry yeast, salt, sugar, and garlic powder. Shake the mixture and add flour. After this, add the boiling water and knead the non-sticky dough. Leave the dough in a warm place for 10 min. Then roll the stick

from the dough and cut it into 4 small logs. Make the pretzels and brush them with the olive oil. Preheat the air fryer to 360 F. Put the pretzels in the air fryer basket and cook for 4 min. When the pretzels are cooked – let them chill gently.

NUTRITION:
calories 131, fat 2.6, fiber 1, carbs 23.5, protein 3.3

CINNAMON APPLE RINGS

Prep time: 10 min | Cooking time: 8 min | Servings: 2

INGREDIENTS:

2 apples
½ tsp ground cinnamon
1 tsp brown sugar
1 tsp olive oil

DIRECTIONS:
Wash the apples carefully and remove the seeds to make the holes in the apples. Then slice the apples. You should get the shape of rings. Preheat the air fryer to 360 F. Place the apple rings in the air fryer basket and spray with the olive oil. Cook for 8 min. Shake the apple rings every 2 min. Meanwhile, combine together the ground cinnamon and brown sugar. Shake the mixture. When the apple rings are cooked – toss them in the sugar mixture and shake well.

NUTRITION:
calories 143, fat 2.7, fiber 5.7, carbs 32.7, protein 0.6

PEPPER CORN FRITTERS

Prep time: 10 min | Cooking time: 12 min | Servings: 2

INGREDIENTS:

4 tbsp flour
2 oz sweet corn kernels
1/3 tsp sugar
1 pinch salt
¼ tsp ground

black pepper
1 tbsp cream
1 egg
½ tsp olive oil

DIRECTIONS:
Separate the egg yolk and egg white. Whisk the egg yolk and combine together with the cream. Add sugar, ground black pepper, and flour. After this, add corn kernels and mix the mixture. Whisk the egg white till the strong peaks. Add the egg white to the dough and mix it up. Preheat the air fryer to 370 F. Spray the air fryer basket with the olive oil inside. Then separate the dough into 2 servings. Pour the first serving in the air fryer basket and cook for 3 min from each side. Repeat the same steps with the second serving. Serve the cooked fritters immediately.

NUTRITION:
calories 237, fat 5.7, fiber 4.7, carbs 42.1, protein 9.5

CHEDDAR HOT DOGS

Prep time: 10 min | Cooking time: 9 min | Servings: 2

INGREDIENTS:

2 hot dog buns
4 Cheddar cheese slices
2 pork sausages
2 tsp pesto sauce

DIRECTIONS:
Preheat the air fryer to 375 F. Put the sausages in the air fryer basket and cook for 8 min. Meanwhile, spread the hot dog buns with the pesto sauce. Then transfer the cooked sausages in the hot dog buns. Place the cheese slices over the sausages. Put the hot dogs in the air fryer basket and cook for 1 min at 400 F. Serve the cooked meal immediately.

NUTRITION:
calories 480, fat 30.4, fiber 0.1, carbs 26.1, protein 22.7

KALE CHIPS
Prep time: 8 min | Cooking time: 4 min | Servings: 2

INGREDIENTS:

7 oz kale
1 tsp dried oregano
1 tsp dried dill
¼ tsp salt
1 tsp garlic powder
1 tbsp olive oil
1 tsp nutritional yeast

DIRECTIONS:
Place the kale in the bowl. Sprinkle it with the dried oregano, dried dill, salt, garlic powder, and nutritional yeast. Mix the kale carefully and add olive oil. Mix it carefully again. Preheat the air fryer to 375 F. Put the kale in the air fryer basket and cook for 4 min. Shake the kale during cooking. Chill the cooked kale and serve.

NUTRITION:
calories 123, fat 7.2, fiber 2.4, carbs 12.9, protein 4.2

CORIANDER SHRIMP CAKES
Prep time: 15 min | Cooking time: 6 min | Servings: 2

INGREDIENTS:

6 oz shrimps, peeled
1 tsp ground coriander
2 tbsp semolina
1 egg
1 tbsp fresh parsley,
chopped
¼ tsp chili flakes
1 tsp butter
½ tsp salt
1 tbsp oatmeal flour

DIRECTIONS:
Chop the peeled shrimps into the tiny pieces. Crack the egg in the chopped shrimps. Add semolina, chopped fresh parsley, ground coriander, chili flakes, salt, and oatmeal flour. Mix the shrimp mixture carefully until homogenous. Then preheat the air fryer to 400 F. Melt the butter in the air fryer basket. Make medium shrimp cakes and put them in the melted butter. Cook the shrimp cakes for 3 min on each side. When the shrimp cakes are cooked – chill them and serve.

NUTRITION:
calories 188, fat 5.7, fiber 0.5, carbs 9.2, protein 23.5

CRUNCHY AVOCADO STICKS
Prep time: 15 min | Cooking time: 9 min | Servings: 2

INGREDIENTS:

1 egg white
1/3 cup panko breadcrumbs
1 tsp olive oil
1 avocado,
pitted
½ tsp salt
½ tsp ground black pepper

DIRECTIONS:
Peel the avocado and cut it into the medium sticks. Then whisk the egg white gently. Place the avocado sticks in the egg white and stir well. Then combine together panko bread crumbs, salt, and ground black pepper. Coat the avocado sticks in the panko breadcrumbs. Preheat the air fryer to 400 F. Put the avocado sticks in the air fryer rack and spray them with the olive oil. Cook the avocado sticks for 9 min. Flip the avocado sticks in halfway of cooking. Serve the avocado sticks warm.

NUTRITION:
calories 306, fat 22.9, fiber 7.7, carbs 22.1, protein 6.2

PICKLES IN PAPRIKA
Prep time: 10 min | Cooking time: 8 min | Servings: 2

INGREDIENTS:

11 oz pickles
4 tbsp flour
¼ tsp baking soda
½ tsp salt
1 tbsp beer
2 tbsp water
4 tbsp panko breadcrumbs
1 tsp paprika

DIRECTIONS:

Slice the pickles and dry them well. Then combine together the flour, baking soda, salt, beer, and water. Stir the mixture until homogenous. Then dip the pickles slices in the flour mixture. Combine the panko breadcrumbs and paprika in the separate bowl. Then coat the pickles slices with the panko breadcrumbs. Preheat the air fryer to 365 F. Place the pickles onto the air fryer rack and cook for 8 min. Flip the pickles after 5 min of cooking. When the pickles are cooked – let them chill gently and serve.

NUTRITION:

calories 105, fat 1.3, fiber 3.1, carbs 20.1, protein 3.3

BACON EGGS

Prep time: 10 min | Cooking time: 10 min | Servings: 2

INGREDIENTS:

4 eggs, boiled
4 bacon slices
1 tsp olive oil
½ tsp salt
½ tsp ground white pepper

DIRECTIONS:

Peel the eggs. Sprinkle the bacon slices with the olive oil, salt, and ground white pepper. Then wrap the eggs in the bacon slices and secure every egg with 1 toothpick. Preheat the air fryer to 380 F. Put the bacon eggs in the air fryer basket and cook for 10 min. Shake the eggs after 5 min of cooking.

NUTRITION:

calories 353, fat 27, fiber 0.1, carbs 1.6, protein 25.2

PARMESAN ZUCCHINI CHIPS

Prep time: 10 min | Cooking time: 8 min | Servings: 2

INGREDIENTS:

1 zucchini
3 oz Parmesan, shredded
1 tbsp Italian seasoning
5 tbsp panko
breadcrumbs
1 tbsp olive oil
½ tsp ground paprika
1 egg, beaten

DIRECTIONS:

Slice the zucchini and dry the zucchini slices. The zucchini slices should be very thin. Combine together panko breadcrumbs and Italian seasoning. Add ground paprika and stir the mixture gently. Whisk the egg. Dip the zucchini slices in the whisked egg. After this, coat the zucchini with the panko breadcrumbs. Preheat the air fryer to 360 F. Put the zucchini slices in the air fryer basket and cook for 7 min. Shake the zucchini slices in halfway. Sprinkle the chips with the shredded cheese and cook for 1 min more.

NUTRITION:

calories 311, fat 21, fiber 2.5, carbs 15.4, protein 19

FIGS WITH GOAT CHEESE

Prep time: 10 min | Cooking time: 7 min | Servings: 2

INGREDIENTS:

3 oz goat cheese
4 figs
½ tsp minced garlic
1 tbsp olive oil
1 tbsp fresh lemon juice
½ tsp ground ginger

DIRECTIONS:

Make the cross cuts in the figs. Remove ½ of all flesh from the figs. Combine the minced garlic, olive oil, and ground ginger in the bowl. Stir the mixture. Add the goat cheese and stir it. Then fill the figs with the goat cheese mixture well. Preheat the air fryer to 360 F and put the figs in the air fryer basket. Sprinkle the figs with the fresh lemon juice and cook for 7 min.

NUTRITION:
calories 351, fat 22.6, fiber 3.8, carbs 25.9, protein 14.4

PAPRIKA CHICKEN BITES
Prep time: 10 min | Cooking time: 8 min | Servings: 2

INGREDIENTS:

4 tbsp coconut flakes	½ tsp ground white pepper
3 tbsp cream	½ tsp paprika
1 tbsp almond flour	10 oz chicken fillet
1/3 tsp salt	1 tsp olive oil

DIRECTIONS:
Combine together the cream, almond flour, salt, ground white pepper, and paprika. Chop the chicken fillet into big bites. Toss the chicken bites in the cream mixture. Then coat the chicken bites with the coconut flakes. Preheat the air fryer to 400 F. Put the chicken bites in the air fryer basket and sprinkle with the olive oil. Cook the chicken bites for 8 min. Shake the chicken bites in halfway of cooking.

NUTRITION:
calories 360, fat 18.9, fiber 1.6, carbs 3.5, protein 42.4

CELERY PORK BALLS
Prep time: 15 min | Cooking time: 11 min | Servings: 2

INGREDIENTS:

1 tbsp celery root	pork
1 tsp minced garlic	½ tsp salt
1 oz carrot, grated	¼ tsp ground nutmeg
8 oz ground	1 tsp olive oil
	1 tbsp almond flour

DIRECTIONS:
Combine together the celery root, minced garlic, grated carrot, ground pork, salt, ground nutmeg, and almond flour. Mix the mixture until it is smooth. After this, make the small balls from the forcemeat. Preheat the air fryer to 390 F. Place the ground pork balls in the air fryer basket and sprinkle them with the olive oil. Cook the meatballs for 11 min. When the meatballs are cooked – they will have little bit crunchy surface.

NUTRITION:
calories 215, fat 8.1, fiber 0.9, carbs 3.2, protein 30.7

SPINACH FRITTERS
Prep time: 12 min | Cooking time: 8 min | Servings: 2

INGREDIENTS:

4 oz spinach	½ tsp salt
1 tbsp olive oil	3 oz ground chicken
1 egg	
3 tbsp semolina	3 tbsp water
2 tbsp flour	1 tsp turmeric

DIRECTIONS:
Chop the spinach and put it in the bowl. Beat the egg in the spinach. Add semolina, flour, salt, ground chicken, and turmeric. Add water and knead the fritters dough. Preheat the air fryer to 376 F. Make the medium fritters from the spinach mixture and place them in the air fryer. Sprinkle the fritters with the olive oil and cook for 4 min from each side.

NUTRITION:
calories 274, fat 12.9, fiber 2.3, carbs 20.3, protein 19.6

DILL RADISH FRIES

Prep time: 10 min | Cooking time: 18 min | Servings: 2

INGREDIENTS:

10 oz radish	1 tsp olive oil
1 tsp dried dill	½ tsp salt

DIRECTIONS:
Wash the radish carefully and cut it into the halves. Sprinkle the radish halves with the dried dill, olive oil, and salt. Shake the radish well. Preheat the air fryer to 370 F. Put the radish in the air fryer and cook for 18 min. Shake the radish 3 times during cooking.

NUTRITION:
calories 44, fat 2.5, fiber 2.3, carbs 5.1, protein 1.1

BEEF BURGERS

Prep time: 15 min | Cooking time: 16 min | Servings: 2

INGREDIENTS:

4 tbsp corn flakes crumbs	beef
1 tsp ground paprika	½ tsp onion powder
¼ tsp ground ginger	½ tsp garlic powder
1 tsp olive oil	1 egg
8 oz minced	½ tsp salt

DIRECTIONS:
Combine together the ground paprika, ground ginger, minced beef, onion powder, garlic powder, and salt. Then beat the egg into the bowl and whisk it. Make 2 medium burgers from the minced beef mixture. Dip the beef burgers in the whisked egg. Then sprinkle the burgers with the corn flakes crumbs. Preheat the air fryer to 370 F. Put the burgers in the air fryer and sprinkle them with the olive oil. Cook the meal for 16 min. Flip the burgers into another side after 8 min of cooking. When the meal is cooked – enjoy it!

NUTRITION:
calories 270, fat 11.8, fiber 0.5, carbs 1.9, protein 37.5

CILANTRO EGGPLANT CHIPS

Prep time: 10 min | Cooking time: 13 min | Servings: 2

INGREDIENTS:

1 eggplants	1 egg
1 tbsp dried cilantro	1 tsp olive oil
½ tbsp paprika	½ tsp salt

DIRECTIONS:
Wash the eggplant carefully and cut it into the chips. Beat the egg in the bowl and whisk it. Then sprinkle the eggplant chips with the whisked egg. Sprinkle the eggplant with the dried cilantro, paprika, and salt. Mix the eggplants carefully. Preheat the air fryer to 400 F. Place the eggplant chips in the air fryer basket and cook for 13 min. The time of cooking depends on the size of the chips. Shake the chips after 5 min of cooking.

NUTRITION:
calories 125, fat 5.2, fiber 10.3, carbs 17.3, protein 5.7

CHICKEN MINI PIES

Prep time: 15 min | Cooking time: 12 min | Servings: 2

INGREDIENTS:

½ onion, sautéed	7 oz ground chicken

4 oz puff pastry   ¼ tsp ground
1 egg yolk   white pepper
¼ tsp salt   1 tsp olive oil

DIRECTIONS:
Roll the puff pastry and cut it into 2 squares. Whisk the egg yolk. Combine together ground chicken, onion, salt, and ground white pepper. Then put the ground chicken mixture in the center of puff pastry squares and secure them in the shape of pies. Then brush the mini pies with the whisked egg yolk. Preheat the air fryer to 370 F. Spray the air fryer basket with olive oil inside. Then place the pies in the air fryer and cook for 12 min. When the pies are cooked – serve them and

NUTRITION:
calories 560, fat 33.6, fiber 1.5, carbs 28.6, protein 34.5

CARROT & POTATO BALLS
Prep time: 10 min | Cooking time: 6 min | Servings: 2

INGREDIENTS:

12 oz mashed   grated
potato   1 tbsp flour
1 tbsp fresh   1 tbsp butter
dill, chopped   ½ tsp salt
1 oz carrot,

DIRECTIONS:
Combine together mashed potato, chopped fresh dill, grated carrot, and flour. Add salt and mix the mixture well. Then make the medium balls from the potato mixture. Preheat the air fryer to 400 F. Toss the butter in the air fryer basket and melt it. Add the potato balls in the air fryer basket and cook for 6 min. Stir the potato balls after 3 min of cooking. The potato balls should have light brown color. Serve the potato balls.

NUTRITION:
calories 267, fat 13, fiber 3.2, carbs 34, protein 4.2

PARMESAN CHICKEN STICKS
Prep time: 10 min | Cooking time: 11 min | Servings: 2

INGREDIENTS:

8 oz chicken   1 tbsp cream
fillet   1 tsp oil
½ tsp salt   3 oz Parmesan,
1 tsp curry   shredded
paste

DIRECTIONS:
Slice the chicken into the thick slices. Then combine curry paste and cream together. Whisk it and salt. Then sprinkle the chicken slices with the curry mixture. Preheat the air fryer to 400 F. Put the chicken slices in the air fryer basket and sprinkle with the olive oil. Cook the chicken for 9 min, After this, sprinkle the chicken with the shredded cheese and cook for 2 min more.

NUTRITION:
calories 393, fat 21.6, fiber 0, carbs 2.4, protein 46.7

TURMERIC CARROT BALLS
Prep time: 10 min | Cooking time: 4 min | Servings: 2

INGREDIENTS:

2 carrot, boiled   1 egg white
½ tsp salt   2 tbsp flour
1 tbsp turmeric   1 tsp olive oil
1 tbsp dried   3 tbsp plain
oregano   yogurt

DIRECTIONS:
Grate the carrot and combine it together with the salt, turmeric, dried oregano, egg white, flour, and plain yogurt. Form the small balls from the carrot mixture.

Preheat the air fryer to 400 F. Place the carrot balls in the air fryer and sprinkle them with the olive oil. Cook the carrot balls for 4 min. When the meal is cooked – chill it till the room temperature.

calories 117, fat 3.3, fiber 3.4, carbs 17.4, protein 4.9

CORN APPLE TOTS
Prep time: 15 min | Cooking time: 6 min | Servings: 2

INGREDIENTS:

1 egg	1 tbsp flour
2 tbsp cream	1 tsp cornstarch
1 tbsp sugar	1 tsp olive oil

DIRECTIONS:
Cut the apple into the big cubes. Beat the egg in the bowl and whisk it. Add the cream and sugar in the whisked egg. After this, add flour and cornstarch. Whisk the mixture until homogenous. Preheat the air fryer to 370 F. Spray the air fryer basket with the olive oil inside. Then dip the apple cubes in the cream mixture. Transfer the dipped apples to the air fryer. Cook the apple tots for 6 min. Shake the apples after 3 min of cooking. When the apple tots have light brown color – they are cooked.

NUTRITION:
calories 101, fat 5.2, fiber 0.1, carbs 10.7, protein 3.3

SESAME PORK CUBES
Prep time: 20 min | Cooking time: 10 min | Servings: 2

INGREDIENTS:

1 tbsp soy sauce	1 tsp paprika
1 tsp sesame seeds, roasted	½ tsp sugar
	8 oz pork chops
	1 tbsp sesame

oil
¼ tsp dried   rosemary

DIRECTIONS:
Cut the pork chops into the cubes. Sprinkle the pork cubes with the paprika, sugar, soy sauce, dried rosemary, and sesame oil. Mix the meat carefully. After this, leave the meat for 10 min to marinate. Preheat the air fryer to 400 F. Put the marinated meat in the air fryer basket. Add all the remaining liquid and cook the meat for 10 min. Stir the meat after 6 min of cooking. Sprinkle the pork cubes with the sesame seeds and stir the meat gently one more time.

NUTRITION:
calories 443, fat 35.9, fiber 0.7, carbs 2.7, protein 26.4

PARMESAN EGG CLOUDS
Prep time: 8 min | Cooking time: 4 min | Servings: 2

INGREDIENTS:

2 egg whites	1 oz Parmesan,
¼ tsp olive oil	shredded
¼ tsp salt	

DIRECTIONS:
Pour the egg whites into the bowl and mix them with the help of the hand mixer for 3 min or till you get the stiff peaks. Add salt and stir gently. Preheat the air fryer to 400 F. Spray the air fryer basket with the olive oil inside. Then make the medium clouds from the egg whites and place them in the air fryer basket. Cook the egg whites clouds for 3 min. Then sprinkle the meal with the shredded cheese and cook for 1 min more.

NUTRITION:
calories 68, fat 3.7, fiber 0, carbs 0.8, protein 8.2

BACON MOZZARELLA

Prep time: 10 min | Cooking time: 9 min | Servings: 2

INGREDIENTS:

4 Mozzarella balls	1 tsp dried oregano
4 slices of bacon	¼ tsp ground paprika
1 tsp olive oil	

DIRECTIONS:

Sprinkle the bacon slices with the dried oregano and ground paprika. Wrap Mozzarella balls in the bacon slices and secure with toothpicks. Sprinkle Mozzarella balls with the olive oil. Preheat the air fryer to 375 F and put the balls in the air fryer basket. Cook the snack for 9 min. Shake the snack after 4 min of cooking.

NUTRITION:

calories 507, fat 38.8, fiber 0.4, carbs 2, protein 33.5

CREAMY SALMON PIECES

Prep time: 10 min | Cooking time: 10 min | Servings: 2

INGREDIENTS:

2 tbsp cream	flakes
1 tbsp flour	¼ tsp salt
¼ cup panko breadcrumbs	8 oz salmon fillet
¼ tsp chili	1 tsp olive oil

DIRECTIONS:

Combine together flour and cream. Mix the mixture. Then cut the salmon fillet into 2 pieces. Sprinkle the salmon pieces with the chili flakes and salt. Dip the salmon fillets in the flour mixture. Then coat the salmon pieces in the panko breadcrumbs. Preheat the air fryer to 380 F. Spray the salmon pieces with the olive oil and put in the air fryer basket. Cook the fish for 10 min.

NUTRITION:

calories 227, fat 10.3, fiber 1.1, carbs 10.9, protein 23.5

HOT BEET CHIPS

Prep time: 10 min | Cooking time: 12 min | Servings: 2

INGREDIENTS:

7 oz beets	per
1 tsp chili flakes	1 tsp olive oil
½ tsp red pep-	¼ tsp sage

DIRECTIONS:

Wash the beet carefully and slice into the chips. Sprinkle the beet chips with the chili flakes, red pepper, olive oil, and sage. Mix up the beet chips carefully. Preheat the air fryer to 360 F. Put the beet chips in the air fryer basket in one layer and cook for 10 min. Then shake the chips gently and cook for 2 min more.

NUTRITION:

calories 74, fat 2.6, fiber 2.4, carbs 12.2, protein 2

DESSERTS

SWEET PUMPKIN LOAF
Prep time: 20 min | Cooking time: 20 min | Servings: 2

INGREDIENTS:

½ tsp baking soda	sugar
2 tbsp pump-kin seeds	1 tsp vanilla extract
1 egg	½ tsp olive oil
¼ cup milk	1 tsp fresh lem-on juice
1/3 cup flour	1 tsp lime zest
2 tbsp brown	1 pinch salt

DIRECTIONS:
Combine together baking soda, flour, brown sugar, vanilla extract, fresh lemon juice, lime zest, and salt in the bowl. Beat the egg in the flour mixture. Add milk and stir the mixture gently with the help of the fork. Crush the pumpkin seeds gently and put them in the flour mixture. Then knead the soft and elastic dough. Add more flour if desired. Let the dough rest for 10 min. Preheat the air fryer to 350 F. Spray the loaf tin with the olive oil and put the dough there. Cook the pumpkin seeds loaf for 15 min. After this, reduce the temperature to 320 F and cook the loaf for 5 min more. Check if the meal is cooked – and transfer it to the serving plate. Slice the sweet pumpkin seeds loaf.

NUTRITION:
calories 221, fat 8.2, fiber 1, carbs 28.4, protein 8.1

MILKY EGG CUSTARD
Prep time: 15 min | Cooking time: 20 min | Servings: 2

INGREDIENTS:

1 egg yolk	½ tsp potato starch
¼ cup milk	
1 tsp white sugar	¼ tsp vanilla extract

DIRECTIONS:
Preheat the air fryer to 210 F. Preheat the milk until it starts to boil. Then whisk together the egg yolk and white sugar. Pour the egg yolk mixture into the hot milk slowly. Whisk it constantly. Add vanilla extract and potato starch. Whisk it well until the mixture is homogenous. Pour the egg mixture into 2 ramekins. Place the ramekins in the air fryer basket. Cook the egg custard for 20 min.

NUTRITION:
calories 55, fat 2.9, fiber 0, carbs 4.9, protein 2.4

RAISINS CARROT PIE
Prep time: 20 min | Cooking time: 35 min | Servings: 2

INGREDIENTS:

3 tbsp flour	¼ tsp ground cinnamon
2 oz carrot, grated	1 pinch salt
1 tbsp raisins	2 tsp brown sugar
¼ tsp baking soda	1 egg
½ tsp apple cider vinegar	2 tbsp milk

DIRECTIONS:
Sift the flour into the bowl. Add grated carrot, raisins, baking soda, apple cider vinegar, ground cinnamon, salt, brown sugar, and milk. Stir the mixture gently. Beat the egg in the separate bowl and whisk it. Pour the whisked egg into the flour mixture. Mix it up until homogenous. The mixture should look like a thick batter. Preheat the air fryer to 350 F. Cover the air fryer tray with the parchment and pour the dough there. Cover the dough with the foil. Pin the foil to give the dough

the opportunity to "breath". Put the pie in the air fryer and cook for 35 min. Then discard the foil and cook the pie for 2 min more at 400 F.

calories 119, fat 2.6, fiber 1.3, carbs 19.4, protein 4.9

CRACKER CHEESECAKE
Prep time: 15 min | Cooking time: 17 min | Servings: 2

INGREDIENTS:

1 tsp butter	1 tbsp brown
3 oz graham	sugar
crackers	1 egg
3 oz cream	¼ tsp vanilla
cheese	extract

DIRECTIONS:
Preheat the air fryer to 360 F. Crush the graham crackers and combine them with the butter. Then cover the air fryer tray with the parchment and put the cracker mixture. Press it gently and slide the tray into the air fryer. Cook the cheesecake crust for 2 min. Then beat the egg in the cream cheese. Add brown sugar and vanilla extract. Mix the mixture carefully until smooth. Pour the cream cheese mixture over the cheesecake crust and flatten it with the help of the spatula. Reduce the air fryer temperature to 310 F. Put the cheesecake in the air fryer and cook for 15 min.

NUTRITION:
calories 109, fat 8.8, fiber 0.8, carbs 3.8, protein 5.2

GINGER APRICOT TART
Prep time: 15 min | Cooking time: 10 min | Servings: 2

INGREDIENTS:

2 tbsp butter	4 tbsp flour
1 pinch salt	1 tsp butter
2 tsp sugar	¼ tsp ground
2 big apricots	ginger

DIRECTIONS:
Combine together the butter, flour, and salt in the mixing bowl. Knead the soft, elastic dough. Roll the dough and separate it into 2 parts. Make the rounds from the dough with the help of the cutter. Then halve the apricots and remove the stones from them. Slice the apricots. Place the apricots in the center of the dough. Roll the edges of the tarts. Add ½ tsp of butter on the top of every tart. Then sprinkle the tarts with the ground ginger and sugar. Preheat the air fryer to 360 F. Place the apricot tarts there and cook for 10 min.

NUTRITION:
calories 217, fat 14.8, fiber 1.1, carbs 19.9, protein 2.2

BANANA OATMEAL BITES
Prep time: 10 min | Cooking time: 8 min | Servings: 2

INGREDIENTS:

2 bananas	2 tbsp panko
1 egg white	breadcrumbs
1 tsp coconut	1 tsp ground
sugar	cinnamon
1 tbsp oatmeal	¼ tsp ground
flour	nutmeg

DIRECTIONS:
Peel the bananas and cut them into the bites. Combine together coconut sugar, panko breadcrumbs, ground cinnamon, and ground nutmeg. Then whisk the egg white gently. Coat the banana bites with the oatmeal flour. Then dip them in the whisked egg white. After this, coat the banana bites with the coconut sugar mixture. Place the banana bites in the air fryer bas-

ket. Cook the banana bites at 360 F for 8 min.

NUTRITION:
calories 159, fat 1.1, fiber 4.3, carbs 35.7, protein 4.5

HONEY PUMPKIN DELIGHTS
Prep time: 20 min | Cooking time: 7 min | Servings: 2

INGREDIENTS:

¼ tsp ground anise	cinnamon
¼ tsp vanilla extract	½ tsp ground ginger
2 tsp honey	1 tsp butter
¼ tsp ground	10 oz pumpkin

DIRECTIONS:
Peel the pumpkin and cut it into 4 pieces. Combine together vanilla extract, ground anise, honey, ground cinnamon, ground ginger, and butter, Churn the mixture. Preheat it if desired. Then sprinkle the pumpkin pieces with the spice mixture and leave them for 15 min or till the pumpkin gives the juice. Then preheat the air fryer to 400 F. Put the pumpkin pieces in the air fryer basket. Sprinkle the pumpkin pieces with the remaining juice mixture. Cook the pumpkin pieces for 7 min. Shake the pumpkin pieces after 3 min of cooking. When the pumpkin pieces are cooked – they should be tender. Let the cooked pumpkin pieces cool briefly. Serve the dessert immediately or keep it in the fridge.

NUTRITION:
calories 91, fat 2.4, fiber 4.4, carbs 18, protein 1.7

NUTMEG BLUEBERRY CRUMBLE
Prep time: 15 min | Cooking time: 15 min | Servings: 2

INGREDIENTS:

3 tbsp blueberry	nutmeg
1 tbsp brown sugar	2 tbsp butter, soft
1 tsp lemon juice	4 tbsp flour
¼ tsp ground	¼ tsp olive oil
	2 tsp white sugar

DIRECTIONS:
Mash the blueberries with the help of the fork. Add lemon juice and brown sugar. Mix the mixture up and add ground nutmeg. Then combine together flour, soft butter, and white sugar. Knead the soft dough. Crumble the dough with the help of the fingertips. Separate the crumbled dough into 2 parts. Then cover the cake tin with the parchment. Place the first part of the crumbled dough in the cake tin, After this, spread the blueberry mixture over the dough. Sprinkle the blueberry mixture with the second part of the dough. Preheat the air fryer to 360 F. Put the crumble in the air fryer and cook for 15 min.

NUTRITION:
calories 206, fat 12.4, fiber 0.8, carbs 22.5, protein 1.9

CHERRY CRUST PIE
Prep time: 15 min | Cooking time: 10 min | Servings: 2

INGREDIENTS:

6 oz pie crust, uncooked	1 tsp brown sugar
2 oz cherry, pitted	1 tsp water
	¼ tsp turmeric

DIRECTIONS:
Roll the pie crust and place the cherries there. Sprinkle the cherries with the brown sugar and turmeric. Place the pie in the air fryer basket and sprinkle the

edges of the pie with water. Preheat the air fryer to 360 F. Cook the pie for 10 min.

NUTRITION:
calories 157, fat 5, fiber 2.6, carbs 28, protein 2.6

CREAM CHEESECAKE SOUFFLÉ

Prep time: 15 min | Cooking time: 10 min | Servings: 2

INGREDIENTS:

5 oz cream cheese	sugar
1 egg yolk	½ tsp vanilla extract
1 egg	½ tsp almond flakes
1 tsp butter	
2 tbsp brown	

DIRECTIONS:
Beat the egg in the bowl. Add the egg yolk and brown sugar. Mix the mixture with the help of the hand mixer. Then add butter, cream cheese, and vanilla extract. Mix the mixture with the help of the hand mixer for 2 min at the maximum speed. After this, pour the cream cheese mixture into 2 ramekins. Preheat the air fryer to 350 F. Place the ramekins in the air fryer basket and cook for 10 min. The soufflé is cooked when you get the light brown color of the surface. Let the soufflé chill for 5 min. Then sprinkle the soufflé with the almond flakes.

NUTRITION:
calories 363, fat 31.3, fiber 0.1, carbs 11.4, protein 9.6

CREAMY CHOCOLATE PROFITEROLES

Prep time: 15 min | Cooking time: 10 min | Servings: 2

INGREDIENTS:

3 tbsp flour	1 tbsp butter
1 egg	2 tbsp whipped cream
2 tbsp water	

DIRECTIONS:
Boil the water and melt the butter. Combine together boiled water, butter, and flour. Mix the mixture and beat the egg. Then mix the dough with the help of the mixer. When you get the plastic dough – transfer it to the pastry bag. Preheat the air fryer to 360 F. Make the profiteroles with the help of the special nozzle and transfer them in the air fryer basket. Cook the profiteroles for 10 min, then chill the profiteroles and cut them crosswise. Fill the profiteroles with the whipped cream.

NUTRITION:
calories 338, fat 25.4, fiber 0.6, carbs 19.1, protein 8 .7

OATS COOKIES

Prep time: 10 min | Cooking time: 9 min | Servings: 2

INGREDIENTS:

3 tbsp oatmeal flour	1 tsp butter
2 tbsp sour cream	1 pinch salt
1 tbsp brown sugar	½ tsp ground cardamom
	1 egg

DIRECTIONS:
Beat the egg in the bowl and whisk it. Add the oatmeal flour and flour in the whisked egg. After this, add sour cream, brown sugar, butter, salt, and ground cardamom. Mix the mixture to get the homogenous dough. Preheat the air fryer to 360 F. Cover the air fryer basket with the parchment. Make the medium cookies from the dough. Use the spoon for this step. Place the cookies in the air fryer basket and cook for 9 min.

NUTRITION:
calories 115, fat 7, fiber 0.8, carbs 9.3, protein 4.2

CHOCOLATE BUTTER BALLS
Prep time: 10 min | Cooking time: 10 min | Servings: 2

INGREDIENTS:

1 tbsp chocolate chips	1 tbsp cocoa powder
1 tbsp butter	¼ tsp vanilla
3 tbsp flour	extract

DIRECTIONS:
Melt the chocolate chips and butter. Combine together the melted ingredients. Then add flour and vanilla extract. Mix the mixture and knead the smooth dough. Make the medium balls from the chocolate mixture. Preheat the air fryer to 360 F. Place the chocolate balls in the air fryer basket and cook for 5 min. After this, reduce the temperature to 345 F and cook the dessert for 5 min more. When the chocolate balls are cooked – sprinkle them with the cocoa powder.

NUTRITION:
calories 129, fat 7.8, fiber 1.3, carbs 13.6, protein 2.2

APRICOT CINNAMON CRUMBLE
Prep time: 15 min | Cooking time: 20 min | Servings: 2

INGREDIENTS:

¼ cup fresh apricot	½ tsp ground cinnamon
1 tbsp brown sugar	3 tbsp flour
1 tbsp butter	1 tsp lime juice

DIRECTIONS:
Halve the apricots and then remove the stones. Then chop the apricots and sprinkle with the ½ tbsp of sugar. Sprinkle the apricots with the lemon juice. Mix the mixture. Then combine together butter, remaining brown sugar, ground cinnamon, and flour. Knead the dough. Then crumble the dough with the help of the fingertips. Put the apricot mixture into the cake tin and spread it well. Then sprinkle the apricots with the crumbled dough. Press it gently. Preheat the air fryer to 360 F. Put the cake tin in the air fryer and cook for 20 min.

NUTRITION:
calories 121, fat 6, fiber 1, carbs 16, protein 1.6

CINNAMON DOUGHNUTS
Prep time: 15 min | Cooking time: 15 min | Servings: 2

INGREDIENTS:

1 tsp sugar	cream
1 tsp butter	1 tsp ground
1/3 cup flour	cinnamon
¼ tsp salt	1 tbsp brown
1 egg yolk	sugar
3 tbsp sour	

DIRECTIONS:
Combine together brown sugar, butter, flour, salt, and sour cream. Knead the smooth and non-sticky dough. Then roll the dough using the rolling pin. After this, use the cutter to make the medium doughnuts. Whisk the egg yolk. Preheat the air fryer to 360 F. Brush the doughnuts with the whisked egg and put in the air fryer. Cook the doughnuts for 15 min. When the surface of the doughnuts is light brown – flip them to another side. Meanwhile, combine together sugar with the cinnamon. When the doughnuts are cooked – sprinkle them gently with the sugar-cinnamon mixture.

calories 186, fat 8.2, fiber 1.2, carbs 24.3, protein 4.2

RAISIN VANILLA MUFFINS
Prep time: 15 min | Cooking time: 10 min | Servings: 2

INGREDIENTS:

1 oz raisins	sugar
¼ cup flour	1 egg
2 tbsp butter	½ tsp vanilla
¼ tsp baking	extract
soda	1 tsp apple
1 tbsp brown	cider vinegar

DIRECTIONS:
Preheat the air fryer to 360 F. Combine together flour, baking soda, and brown sugar. Then add raisins, butter, vanilla extract, and apple cider vinegar. Crack the egg into the mixture. Take the fork and mix the mixture well. Then use the hand mixer to make the homogenous mass. The dough should be liquid as a batter. Pour the muffin dough into the muffin molds. Place the muffin molds in the air fryer basket. Cook the muffins for 10 min or until the top of the muffins are light brown.

NUTRITION:
calories 253, fat 13.9, fiber 0.9, carbs 27.9, protein 5

CHOCOLATE CHIP MUFFINS
Prep time: 15 min | Cooking time: 10 min | Servings: 2

INGREDIENTS:

2 oz chocolate	cream
chips	1 tsp cocoa
2 oz butter	powder
1 egg	1/3 cup flour
1 tsp vanilla	1 tbsp sugar
extract	1 tsp lemon
1 tsp sour	juice

DIRECTIONS:
Make the butter soft and combine it with the vanilla extract and sour cream. Add cocoa powder, flour, sugar, and lemon juice. After this beat the egg in the flour mixture and mix it with the help of the hand mixer until homogenous. Sprinkle the dough with the chocolate chips and stir it carefully. Preheat the air fryer to 365 F. Use the spoon to fill the muffin molds with the dough. Put the muffin molds in the air fryer basket. Cook the muffins for 10 min. Then check if the muffins are cooked using the toothpick

NUTRITION:
calories 498, fat 34.4, fiber 1.8, carbs 39.8, protein 7.6

COCOA BROWNIES
Prep time: 15 min | Cooking time: 15 min | Servings: 2

INGREDIENTS:

3 tbsp cocoa	3 tbsp flour
powder	4 tbsp butter,
1 tbsp nuts,	soft
crushed	2 tbsp brown
1 pinch salt	sugar
1 egg	

DIRECTIONS:
Beat the egg in the mixing bowl and whisk it. Combine the cocoa powder, salt, flour, and brown sugar in the separate bowl. Stir the mixture. Put the dried mixture in the mixing bowl. Add crushed nuts. Melt the butter and pour it into the mixture. Mix it up to make the smooth dough. Preheat the air fryer to 350 F. Pour the brownie dough into the air fryer tray and flatten it gently with the help of the spatula. Cook the brownie for 15 min. Check if the brownie is cooked and remove it from the air fryer.

Place the brownie on the chopping plate. Cut it into the serving pieces.

NUTRITION:
calories 355, fat 28.6, fiber 3.1, carbs 23.5, protein 6.4

WALNUT BAKED APPLES
Prep time: 15 min | Cooking time: 20 | Servings: 2

INGREDIENTS:

2 apples	1 tsp ground
2 tsp walnuts,	ginger
crushed	2 tsp butter
2 tsp ground	2 tsp honey
cinnamon	1 tsp vanilla
2 tsp brown	extract
sugar	

DIRECTIONS:
Make the small holes in the apples and remove the seeds. Combine the crushed walnuts, ground cinnamon, brown sugar, ground ginger, butter, honey, and vanilla extract. Mix the mixture carefully. Then fill the apple holes with the walnut mixture. Preheat the air fryer to 350 F. Put the apples in the air fryer basket and cook 20 min.

NUTRITION:
calories 213, fat 5.8, fiber 6.9, carbs 42.5, protein 1.

NUTMEG APRICOT MUFFINS
Prep time: 15 min | Cooking time: 12 min | Servings: 2

INGREDIENTS:

1 tbsp apricot	3 tbsp butter
jam	½ tsp baking
2 apricots	soda
½ tsp ground	1 tsp vanilla
nutmeg	extract
1 tsp lemon	3 tbsp brown
juice	sugar
5 tbsp flour	

DIRECTIONS:
Halve the apricots and remove the stones. Chop the apricots and combine them with the jam. Add brown sugar, lemon juice, ground nutmeg, baking soda, and vanilla extract. Mix the mixture up and add flour. Then melt the butter and add it to the ham mixture. Use the hand mixer to make the homogenous dough. Preheat the air fryer to 360 F. Fill ½ part of every muffin mold with the dough and place them in the air fryer basket. Cook the muffins for 12 min. When the muffins are cooked – let them chill briefly and remove from the air fryer basket.

NUTRITION:
calories 326, fat 17.9, fiber 1.4, carbs 39, protein 2.8

CAKE WITH VANILLA FROSTING
Prep time: 20 min | Cooking time: 25 min | Servings: 2

INGREDIENTS:

¼ cup flour	¼ cup sugar
2 tbsp butter	4 tbsp heavy
1 egg	cream
½ tsp vanilla	2 tbsp brown
extract	sugar

DIRECTIONS:
Separate the egg yolk and egg white. Whisk the egg yolks with the sugar until you get the lemon color mixture. Then add butter and flour. Whisk the egg white until the strong peaks. Then add the egg white to the egg yolk mixture. Stir it carefully with the help of the spatula. Preheat the air fryer to 360 F. Transfer the dough to the air fryer cake tin and slice it in the air fryer. Cook the sponge cake for 15 min. After this, reduce the air fryer

temperature to 350 F and cook the cake for 10 min more. Meanwhile, make the frosting: whisk together brown sugar and heavy cream. When the sponge cake is cooked – transfer it to the serving plate and spread with the frosting.

NUTRITION:
calories 425, fat 25, fiber 0.4, carbs 46.9, protein 5.1

MARSHMALLOW & BUTTER BANANAS
Prep time: 10 min | Cooking time: 5 min | Servings: 2

INGREDIENTS:

2 bananas	butter
2 tbsp mini marshmallow	¼ tsp ground cinnamon
2 tsp peanut	

DIRECTIONS:
Do not peel the bananas and make the crosswise cuts in them. Open the cuts of the bananas to make the pockets. Sprinkle the banana pockets with the ground cinnamon. Then add peanut butter and mini marshmallow. Preheat the air fryer to 400 F. Put the bananas in the air fryer basket and cook for 5 min or until the marshmallow starts to melt and the bananas are soft.

NUTRITION:
calories 183, fat 3.1, fiber 3.6, carbs 39.4, protein 2.7

CHOCOLATE SAUCE
Prep time: 8 min | Cooking time: 4 min | Servings: 2

INGREDIENTS:

3 tbsp chocolate chips	1 tsp butter
2 tbsp heavy cream	1 tbsp milk
	½ tsp vanilla extract

DIRECTIONS:
Melt the butter and combine it with the heavy cream and milk. Add vanilla extract and mix the mixture. Preheat the air fryer to 400 F. Put the chocolate chips in the air fryer basket and cook them for 2 min. When the chocolate chips are melted – add the heavy cream mixture. Cook the mixture for 2 min more. After this, stir the mixture with the help of the spatula and cook it for 2 min more. Stir it carefully until the sauce is homogenous. Pour the sauce into the ramekins and serve.

NUTRITION:
calories 160, fat 12.3, fiber 0.5, carbs 10.3, protein 1.8

APPLE PASTRIES
Prep time: 15 min | Cooking time: 8 min | Servings: 2

INGREDIENTS:

1 red apples	cinnamon
2 tsp brown sugar	2 tsp butter
1 tsp ground	3 oz puff pastry
	1 egg yolk

DIRECTIONS:
Roll the puff pastry and cut it into 2 squares. Roll the edges of the squares. Then halve the apple and slice it. Place the apple slices in the center of dough squares. Then sprinkle the apples with the ground cinnamon, sugar, and butter. Whisk the egg yolk and brush the dough edges. Preheat the air fryer to 400 F. Cover the air fryer basket with the parchment and put the pastries there. Cook the dessert for 8 min or until it is cooked.

NUTRITION:
calories 367, fat 22.5, fiber 4, carbs 38.8, protein 4.8

CASHEW COOKIES
Prep time: 15 min | Cooking time: 15 min | Servings: 2

INGREDIENTS:

3 tbsp flour	extract
1 tsp butter	1 tbsp brown
1 tsp cashew,	sugar
crushed	½ tsp cream
½ tsp vanilla	

DIRECTIONS:
Make the butter soft and place it in the big bowl. Add flour and vanilla extract. After this, add brown sugar and cream. Knead the smooth and non-sticky dough. Roll the dough and make the cookies with the help of the cutter. Sprinkle every cookie with the crushed cashews. Press the surface of the cookies lightly. Preheat the air fryer to 360 F. Put the cookies in the air fryer basket tray and cook the cookies for 15 min. When the cookies are cooked – let them chill briefly.

NUTRITION:
calories 88, fat 2.7, fiber 0.4, carbs 14, protein 1.5

VANILLA OAT ROLLS
Prep time: 15 min | Cooking time: 17 min | Servings: 2

INGREDIENTS:

¼ tsp active yeast	2 tsp butter
3 tsp brown	4 tbsp flour
sugar	1 tsp oatmeal
1 tsp vanilla	flour
sugar	1 pinch salt
1 tsp vanilla	½ tsp olive oil
extract	2 tbsp cream

DIRECTIONS:
Preheat the cream to the room temperature and combine it with the active yeast. Stir it carefully until the yeast is dissolved. Then add brown sugar, vanilla extract, flour, and oatmeal flour. Add salt and knead the soft but non-sticky dough. Roll the dough and sprinkle it with the vanilla sugar. The roll up the dough and cut it into rolls. Sprinkle the vanilla rolls with the olive oil. Preheat the air fryer to 365 F. Put the vanilla rolls in the air fryer and cook them for 17 min. Check the doneness of the rolls after 13 min of cooking.

NUTRITION:
calories 143, fat 5.9, fiber 0.6, carbs 19.6, protein 2.1

CHOCOLATE VANILLA SOUF-FLE
Prep time: 15 min | Cooking time: 15 min | Servings: 2

INGREDIENTS:

2 oz dark chocolate	1 oz sugar
	¼ tsp vanilla
3 tbsp butter	extract
2 eggs	2 tsp sugar,
1 oz flour	powdered

DIRECTIONS:
Separate the egg yolks and egg whites. Whisk the egg yolks with the sugar and vanilla extract. Then melt the butter and dark chocolate. Combine the butter and dark chocolate together. Pour the mixture into the egg yolks and stir it. Add flour and mix it until homogenous. Then whisk the egg whites until the strong peaks. Pour the chocolate mixture into the ramekins. Then add the egg white mixture and stir it gently. Preheat the air fryer to 330 F. Put the ramekins in the air fryer basket and cook for 15 min. When the soufflé is cooked let it chill briefly. Sprinkle the surface of the soufflé with the powdered sugar.

NUTRITION:
calories 483, fat 30.2, fiber 1.3, carbs 44.7, protein 9.4

ALMOND BARS

Prep time: 15 min | Cooking time: 12 min | Servings: 2

INGREDIENTS:

2 tbsp sugar, powdered	3 tbsp almond flour
¼ tsp baking powder	2 oz almonds, crushed
3 tbsp butter, soft	½ tsp olive oil

DIRECTIONS:
Combine together the soft butter, baking powder, powdered sugar, almond flour, and olive oil. Knead the plastic dough. Place the dough in the air fryer basket and sprinkle over with the crushed almonds. Press the crushed almonds gently. After this, preheat the air fryer to 360 F. Cook the almond bar for 12 min. After this, transfer the cooked almond bar into the serving plate. Cut it into the servings. Enjoy the almond bars immediately or keep them in the paper bags.

NUTRITION:
calories 435, fat 37.6, fiber 14.7, carbs 20.6, protein 8.4

BANANA PASTRIES

Prep time: 15 min | Cooking time: 6 min | Servings: 2

INGREDIENTS:

1 banana	extract
2 filo sheets	1 tbsp water
1 tsp butter, melted	¼ tsp ground nutmeg
¼ tsp vanilla	

DIRECTIONS:
Peel the banana and chop it. Combine the chopped banana

with the vanilla extract and ground nutmeg. Then place together filo sheets and roll them. Cut the filo sheets into 2 pieces. Place the banana filling on the filo sheets and secure them to make the pastries. Preheat the air fryer to 350 F. Sprinkle the banana pastries with the water and put them in the air fryer basket. Cook the pastries for 6 min.

NUTRITION:
calories 72, fat 2.2, fiber 1.6, carbs 13.7, protein 0.7

BANANA CINNAMON CAKE

Prep time: 10 min | Cooking time: 7 min | Servings: 2

INGREDIENTS:

2 bananas	2 tsp white sugar
2 eggs	
1 tbsp oatmeal flour	¼ tsp ground cinnamon
1 tsp butter	

DIRECTIONS:
Peel the bananas and mash them with the help of the fork. Beat the eggs in the mashed banana. Add oatmeal flour, butter, white sugar, and ground cinnamon. Mix the banana mixture with the help of the hand mixer. After this, preheat the air fryer to 365 F. Pour the mashed banana mixture into the air fryer basket and flatten it gently. Cook the banana cake for 7 min. The cooked cake should be very soft.

NUTRITION:
calories 208, fat 6.8, fiber 3.5, carbs 32.8, protein 7.2

CARAMEL POPCORN

Prep time: 10 min | Cooking time: 15 min | Servings: 2

INGREDIENTS:

| 1 cup corn kernels | 1 tsp olive oil |
| | 2 tbsp caramel |

DIRECTIONS:
Preheat the air fryer to 450 F. Place the baking cage in the air fryer basket. Put the corn kernels in the baking cage. Cook the popcorn for 5 min. After this, transfer the cooked popcorn to the bowl. Sprinkle it with the caramel and shake well. Spray the air fryer basket with the olive oil inside. Put the caramel popcorn in the air fryer basket and cook it at 250 F for 10 min. Shake the cooked poporn carefully and serve.

NUTRITION:
calories 88, fat 3.3, fiber 2.1, carbs 14.7, protein 2.5

CHOCOLATE SUGARY CUP-CAKES
Prep time: 15 min | Cooking time: 10 min | Servings: 2

INGREDIENTS:

2 tbsp cocoa powder	sugar
1/3 tsp baking powder	3 tbsp butter
1 tsp apple cider vinegar	5 tbsp flour
2 tsp brown	1 egg
	2 tbsp whipped cream
	½ tsp lime zest

DIRECTIONS:
Beat the egg in the mixing bowl and whisk it. Add baking powder, apple cider vinegar, brown sugar, butter, cocoa powder, and flour. Use the mixer to make the smooth cupcake dough. Preheat the air fryer to 365 F. Pour the cupcake dough into the cupcake molds. Then place the cupcakes in the air fryer basket and cook for 10 min. Cook for 2 extra min of desired. Then remove the cupcakes from the air fryer and chill them well. Sprinkle the cupcakes with the whipped cream. Then

sprinkle the lemon zest over the whipped cream.

NUTRITION:
calories 324, fat 25, fiber 2.2, carbs 21.9, protein 6.3

CINNAMON FRIED BANANAS
Prep time: 10 min | Cooking time: 4 min | Servings: 2

INGREDIENTS:

1 tbsp maple syrup	2 tbsp oatmeal
2 tsp brown sugar	1/3 tsp ground cinnamon
2 tsp butter	1 egg white, whisked
2 bananas	

DIRECTIONS:
Combine the whisked egg white with the brown sugar, ground cinnamon, and maple syrup. Melt the butter and add it to the whisked egg white mixture. Stir it carefully. Peel the bananas and dip them in the egg white mixture. Then sprinkle the bananas with the oatmeal generously. Preheat the air fryer to 400 F. Place the bananas in the air fryer basket and cook for 4 min. Flip the bananas into another side after 2 min of cooking. Serve hot.

NUTRITION:
calories 205, fat 4.6, fiber 3.8, carbs 40.5, protein 3.8

MARBLE COCOA CAKE
Prep time: 20 min | Cooking time: 16 min | Servings: 2

INGREDIENTS:

1 pinch salt	1 tsp cocoa powder
2 tsp white sugar	¼ tsp lemon juice
1 tbsp butter	3 tbsp flour
1 egg	

Directions:
Preheat the air fryer to 360 F. Combine together a ½ tbsp of butter and 1 tsp white sugar. Mix the mixture well until you get the smooth paste. Beat the egg in the separate bowl and whisk it. Then pour ½ part of the whisked egg in the butter paste. Add 1 tbsp of flour, cocoa powder, and a pinch of salt. Then whisk the mixture. Combine together the remaining butter, sugar, flour, and whisked the egg. Add lemon juice and stir it carefully. Transfer the white butter mixture to the air fryer tray. Then pour the chocolate mixture into the center of the white butter mixture. Make the swirls with the help of the wooden stick. Cook the marble cake for 16 min. When the cake is cooked – chill it well.

NUTRITION:
calories 111, fat 6, fiber 0.6, carbs 13.4, protein 1.4

SUGARY FRENCH PALMIER
Prep time: 10 min | Cooking time: 15 min | Servings: 2

INGREDIENTS:

5 oz puff pastry	sugar
2 tsp brown	½ tsp olive oil

DIRECTIONS:
Roll the puff pastry. Make the logs from the puff pastry and sprinkle them with the brown sugar. Then roll the puff pastry logs from 2 sides until they meet each other. Then sprinkle the air fryer basket with the olive oil. Place the palmiers in the air fryer. Cook the dessert for 15 min at 355 F. When French palmiers are cooked – chill them well. Sprinkle the meal with the sugar again if desired.

NUTRITION:
calories 412, fat 28.2, fiber 1.1, carbs 34.9, protein 5.2

CREAMY CHAKALI
Prep time: 20 min | Cooking time: 5 min | Servings: 2

INGREDIENTS:

3 tbsp curd	¼ tsp chili powder
3 tbsp cornstarch	1 tsp sugar
2 tbsp cream	2 tbsp olive oil
1 tbsp flour	

DIRECTIONS:
Combine together the curd, cornstarch, cream, chili powder, sugar, and olive oil. Knead the smooth and non-sticky dough. Place it in the fridge for 10 min. After this, place the dough in the pastry bag. Make the medium cookies with the help of the round nozzle. Place the chakali on the parchment. Preheat the air fryer to 360 F. Place the parchment with the chakali in the air fryer basket. Cook the chakali for 5 min.

NUTRITION:
calories 202, fat 15.6, fiber 0.2, carbs 14, protein 2.6

VANILLA BREAD PUDDING
Prep time: 15 min | Cooking time: 6 min | Servings: 2

INGREDIENTS:

1 tbsp cream	extract
2 eggs	1 tbsp butter
5 oz white bread	2 tsp brown sugar
1 tsp vanilla	

DIRECTIONS:
Beat the eggs in the bowl and whisk. Chop the white bread into the tiny pieces and combine with the whisked egg. Add cream, va-

nilla extract, butter, and brown sugar. Mix the mixture carefully until homogenous. Preheat the air fryer to 360 F. Pour the bread mixture into the air fryer basket and cook for 6 min. When the pudding is cooked – the surface should be light brown.

NUTRITION:
calories 324, fat 12.8, fiber 1.7, carbs 39.6, protein 11.1

OAT CHOCOLATE CHIP COOKIES
Prep time: 10 min | Cooking time: 7 min | Servings: 2

INGREDIENTS:

1 tbsp chocolate chips	1 tsp lemon zest
3 tbsp flour	¼ tsp vanilla sugar
3 tbsp butter	
1 tbsp oatmeal	

DIRECTIONS:
Melt the butter and combine it together with the chocolate chips and flour. Add oatmeal, lemon zest, and vanilla sugar. Mix the mixture carefully with the help of the spoon and then knead it with the help of the fingertips. Make the medium balls from the dough and flatten them gently in the shape of the cookies. Preheat the air fryer to 365 F. Place the cookies in the air fryer basket and cook for 7 min. The time of cooking depends on the size of the cookies. When the cookies are cooked – let them chill well and serve.

NUTRITION:
calories 236, fat 19.1, fiber 0.8, carbs 14.5, protein 2.2

BANANA PUFF ROLLS
Prep time: 15 min | Cooking time: 12 min | Servings: 2

INGREDIENTS:

4 oz puff pastry	balls
1 banana	2 tsp butter
2 ice cream	2 tsp water
	½ tbsp sugar

DIRECTIONS:
Peel the banana and mash it with the help of the fork. Roll the puff pastry and spread it with the mashed banana. Melt the butter and combine it with the sugar. Sprinkle the mashed banana with the melted butter mixture. After this, roll the puff pastry and cut it into 2 servings. Preheat the air fryer to 365 F. Sprinkle the banana rolls with water and place it in the air fryer basket. Cook the banana rolls for 12 min. Placed the cooked banana rolls on the serving plates. The cooked meal should be a little bit crunchy. Place the ice cream balls on the banana rolls and serve them.

NUTRITION:
calories 547, fat 32.6, fiber 2.9, carbs 58.1, protein 7.1

APPLE PASTRY DUMPLINGS
Prep time: 15 min | Cooking time: 20 min | Servings: 2

INGREDIENTS:

1 green apple	1 tsp butter
1 egg yolk	¼ tsp turmeric
2 tsp brown sugar	6 oz puff pastry

DIRECTIONS:
Chop the green apple into the small pieces. Combine together the chopped apple, butter, brown sugar, and turmeric. Shake the mixture well. Roll the puff pastry with the help of the rolling pin and cut it into the squares. After this, place the apple mixture in the center of every square and wrap them in the shape of the

dumpling. Whisk the egg yolk and brush the dumplings. Preheat the air fryer to 357 F. Place the dumplings in the air fryer and cook for 20 min.

NUTRITION:
calories 583, fat 6.8, fiber 4, carbs 57.2, protein 7.9

NY CREAM CHEESECAKE
Prep time: 15 min | Cooking time: 37 min | Servings: 2

INGREDIENTS:

2 eggs	¼ tsp vanilla
7 oz cream	extract
cheese	4 tbsp flour
2 tbsp sugar,	2 tbsp butter
powdered	

DIRECTIONS:
Beat the eggs in the bowl and whisk them together with the cream cheese and powdered sugar. After this, combine together flour and 1 tbsp of butter. Knead the soft, non-sticky dough. Place the dough in the air fryer cake tin and flatten it in the shape of the cheesecake crust. Preheat the air fryer to 360 F and cook the crust for 12 min. After this, remove the cheesecake crust from the air fryer and crumble it well. Then combine the crumbled cheesecake crust with the remaining butter and make the homogenous mass. Place the mass in the air fryer cake tin again. Then flatten it well. Pour the cream cheese mixture over the cheesecake crust and flatten it with the help of the plastic spatula. Cook the cheesecake for 25 min at 360 F. When the cheesecake is cooked chill it for at least 2 h.

NUTRITION:
calories 614, fat 50.6, fiber 0.4, carbs 27, protein 14.8

CINNAMON CHURROS
Prep time: 10 min | Cooking time: 6 min | Servings: 2

INGREDIENTS:
¼ cup water, hot

1 egg	1 tbsp brown
1 pinch salt	sugar
1/3 cup flour	1 tsp ground
1 tbsp butter	cinnamon

DIRECTIONS:
Combine together flour, butter, salt, and hot water. Mix the mixture until smooth. Then beat the egg in the flour mixture and mix it with the help of the hand mixer. Fill the piping bag with the dough. Cover the air fryer basket with the parchment. Make the small sticks (churros) from the dough. Preheat the air fryer to 400 F and cook the meal for 6 min. Meanwhile, combine together the brown sugar and ground cinnamon. Toss the cooked churros to the sugar mixture and coat well.

NUTRITION:
calories 178, fat 8.2, fiber 1.2, carbs 21.4, protein 5

BANANA BREAD
Prep time: 15 min | Cooking time: 25 min | Servings: 2

INGREDIENTS:

4 tbsp flour	¼ tsp baking
2 banana	soda
1 egg	2 tsp brown
3 tbsp cream	sugar

DIRECTIONS:
Peel the bananas and mash them. Combine together the mashed bananas and flour. Beat the egg in the banana mixture. Add cream, baking soda, and brown sugar. Mix the mixture well. Take the loaf mold and transfer the dough

there. Preheat the air fryer to 360 F. Place the loaf mold in the air fryer and cook for 10 min. After this, reduce the temperature to 350 F and cook the banana bread for 15 min more. When the banana bread is cooked – discard it from the mold and chill it well.

NUTRITION:
calories 216, fat 3.7, fiber 3.5, carbs 42.6, protein 5.8

APPLE PASTRY ROSES
Prep time: 10 min | Cooking time: 7 min | Servings: 2

INGREDIENTS:

1 apple
3 oz puff pastry
1 tbsp white
sugar
1 tsp butter

DIRECTIONS:
Roll out the dough thinly. Slice the apple thinly. Then place the sliced apples over the dough. Roll the dough into the medium roses. Preheat the air fryer to 360 F. Spread the air fryer basket with the butter and put the roses there. Cook the apple roses for 7 min.

NUTRITION:
calories 332, fat 18.3, fiber 3.3, carbs 40.6, protein 3.4

CREAMY CARAMEL MUFFINS
Prep time: 10 min | Cooking time: 12 min | Servings: 2

INGREDIENTS:

1 oz caramel
1 egg
4 oz sour cream
1/3 tsp baking powder
4 tbsp flour
2 tsp white sugar
1 tsp butter

DIRECTIONS:
Beat the egg in the mixing bowl and whisk it. Add sour cream and baking powder. After this, add flour, white sugar, and butter. Use the mixer to make the smooth mass. Then pour the dough into the muffin molds. Fill the piping bag with the caramel. Fill the muffin dough with the caramel. Preheat the air fryer to 365 F. Place the muffins in the air fryer basket and cook them for 12 min.

NUTRITION:
calories 296, fat 17.3, fiber 0.4, carbs 29.8, protein 6.8

MILKY SEMOLINA CAKE
Prep time: 15 min | Cooking time: 6 min | Servings: 2

INGREDIENTS:

4 tbsp semolina
8 tbsp milk
1 tbsp flour
2 tbsp white
sugar
1 tsp butter
1 egg yolk
1 tsp vanilla extract

DIRECTIONS:
Combine together semolina and milk. Whisk the egg yolk in the separate bowl. Add flour and white sugar. After this, combine together semolina mixture and egg yolk mixture. Add butter and vanilla extract. Whisk it well. Preheat the air fryer to 400 F. Place the semolina mixture in the air fryer basket and cook it for 6 min. When the cake is cooked – it will have golden brown surface.

NUTRITION:
calories 215, fat 5.7, fiber 0.9, carbs 33.8, protein 6.4

PLUM JAM TARTS
Prep time: 20 min | Cooking time: 15 min | Servings: 2

INGREDIENTS:

¼ tsp active yeast	2 tbsp plum jam
1 pinch salt	¼ cup whey
2 tsp white sugar	6 tbsp flour
	1 tsp butter

DIRECTIONS:
Preheat whey gently and add the active yeast. Whisk the mixture until smooth. Then add salt, white sugar, and flour. Knead the smooth dough. Add more flour if desired. Then roll out the dough. Separate the dough into 2 parts. Take 2 mini cake tins and place the dough there. Leave the dough for 10 min to make it rise. Spread the dough with the jam. Place the butter over the jam. Preheat the air fryer to 365 F. Put the tarts in the air fryer basket. Cook the tarts for 10 min. Then reduce the temperature to 350 F and cook the tarts for 5 min more. Chill the tarts till the room temperature.

NUTRITION:
calories 207, fat 2.6, fiber 1, carbs 42.2, protein 3.8

PUMPKIN EGG MOUSSE
Prep time: 10 min | Cooking time: 13 min | Servings: 2

INGREDIENTS:

6 oz pumpkin puree	sugar
3 egg yolks	1 tbsp butter
2 eggs, beaten	1 tsp pumpkin pie spices
2 tbsp brown	

DIRECTIONS:
Combine together egg yolks and eggs. Mix them carefully with the help of the mixer. Add brown sugar and pumpkin pie spices. Then melt the butter and add it to the egg mixture. Add pumpkin puree and stir it carefully with the help of the spatula. Preheat the air fryer to 350 F. Pour the pumpkin puree mixture into 2 ramekins. Place the ramekins in the air fryer and cook for 13 min. Whisk the mousse every 3 min during cooking.

NUTRITION:
calories 261, fat 17.3, fiber 2.6, carbs 17.6, protein 10.6

STRAWBERRY COBBLER
Prep time: 15 min | Cooking time: 10 min | Servings: 2

INGREDIENTS:

2 tbsp flour	2 tsp white sugar
1 tsp butter	
1 tsp vanilla extract	3 oz strawberries, chopped
1 egg	

DIRECTIONS:
Combine together chopped strawberries and vanilla extract. Add sugar and stir the mixture. Then combine together flour and butter. Beat the egg in the flour mixture and mix it well. Place the strawberry mixture into 2 ramekins. Separate the dough into 2 parts. Roll out the dough into the shape of the ramekins. Then cover the strawberries with the dough and secure the edges. Make the X cut in the center of the dough. Cover the ramekins with the foil. Preheat the air fryer to 350 F. Put the ramekins in the air fryer basket and cook the cobbler for 10 min. The discard the foil and chill the meal.

NUTRITION:
calories 111, fat 4.3, fiber 1.1, carbs 13.7, protein 3.9

VANILLA PLUM CRUMBLE
Prep time: 20 min | Cooking time: 22 min | Servings: 2

INGREDIENTS:

4 plums, pitted
2 tbsp butter
4 tbsp flour
¼ tsp vanilla extract
2 tbsp brown sugar
1 tbsp sugar, powdered
¼ tsp ground nutmeg

DIRECTIONS:

Chop the plums. Melt the butter and combine it with flour and vanilla extract. Mix the mixture until you get the soft dough. Place the dough in the freezer for 15 min. Meanwhile, combine together the chopped plums and brown sugar. Stir the mixture. Remove the frozen dough from the freezer and grate it. Then separate the dough into parts. Sprinkle the air fryer cake tin with the first part of the dough. Then spread the dough over the chopped plums. Sprinkle the plum surface with the all remaining dough. Preheat the air fryer to 360 F. Cook the crumble for 22 min. When the crumble is cooked – it should be a little bit crunchy. Chill it to the room temperature.

NUTRITION:

calories 278, fat 12.2, fiber 2.3, carbs 43, protein 2.8

CONCLUSION

There are many kitchen appliances that can help you during the day. As every kitchen machine, an air fryer has as advantages as disadvantages. The main positive side of the air fryer is a fast time of cooking. This multi-functional machine can bake, roast, and grill. The kitchen appliance needs only electricity. That is why it becomes very easy to use the air fryer almost everywhere – countryside, forest, or at home.

The air fryer is appropriate for everyone: you can easily entrust cooking as for teenagers, adults, as for old people. This kitchen machine is able to fulfill all your cooking desires instantly!

Nevertheless, the air fryer has two weak sides that are important to know too. Some types of the air fryers have a big size that is not always suited for a small kitchen. So it can take up a lot of space at your house.

Secondly, do not hide that the food that is cooked in air fryer has little bit different taste in comparison the taste of the meal that is cooked by an ordinary method.

The using of air fryer looks very complicated at first sign. Do not be scared! Step by step you will figure out the art of the air fryer cooking!

RECIPE INDEX

Carrot Lentil Burgers, 40
Sugary Carrot Strips, 40
Honey Carrots with Greens, 54
Maple Carrot Fries, 56
Carrot Chips, 57
Carrot & Potato Balls, 66
Turmeric Carrot Balls, 66
Raisins Carrot Pie, 69

CASHEW
Smoked Cashews, 60
Cashew Cookies, 77

CATFISH
Catfish Nuggets, 23
Garlic Catfish, 24
Crunchy Catfish, 26
Catfish Sticks, 55

CAULIFLOWER
Creamy Cauliflower Head, 42
Cream Cheese Cauliflower, 51
Puff Cauliflower Patties, 53
Mayo Cauliflower Florets, 59

CHEDDAR
Avocado Cheddar Rolls, 7
Cheddar Eggs Burrito, 7
Baked Cheddar Eggs, 10
Cheddar Baked Paprika Toasts, 11
Cheddar Hash Browns, 14
Cheddar Bread Pizza, 14
Cheddar Zucchini Frittata, 15
Running Cheddar Eggs, 16
Cheddar Potato Halves, 17
Cheddar Crumpets, 21
Cheddar Chicken Breast, 34
Cheddar Potato Gratin, 39
Cheddar Portobello Mushrooms, 42
Cheddar Mac'n'Cheese, 45
Chard with Cheddar, 49
Cheddar Hot Dogs, 61

CHICKEN
Chicken Sausages, 6
Tabasco Chicken Meatballs, 15
Chicken Mushroom Rolls, 16

Chicken Strips, 17
Paprika Chicken Buns, 21
Pineapple Chicken Breast, 22
Chicken Oatmeal Schnitzel, 25
Garlic Ground Chicken, 26
Celery Chicken Wings, 26
Butter Chicken Drumsticks, 28
Curry Chicken Breast, 28
Onion Chicken Skin, 32
Cheddar Chicken Breast, 34
Yogurt Chicken Kebab, 36
Dijon Chicken, 36
Oat Chicken Sausages, 37
Creamy Chicken Liver, 55
Paprika Chicken Bites, 64
Chicken Mini Pies, 65
Parmesan Chicken Sticks, 66

CHILI
Chili Pork Slices, 32
Coconut Chili Beef Strips, 37
Chili Squash Wedges, 52
Chili Onion Rings, 58

CHOCOLATE
Creamy Choco Profiteroles, 72
Chocolate Butter Balls, 73
Chocolate Chip Muffins, 74
Chocolate Sauce, 76
Chocolate Vanilla Soufflé, 77
Chocolate Sugary Cupcakes, 79
Oat Chocolate Chip Cookies, 81

COCONUT
Coconut Chili Beef Strips, 37

COD
Milky Cod, 16
Italian Beer Cod, 23
Creamy Cod Fillet, 27

CORN
Paprika Corn Beef, 30
Corn on Cobs, 40
Mexican Parmesan Corn, 51
Corn Okra Bites, 57
Corn & Beans Fries, 58
Pepper Corn Fritters, 61
Corn Apple Tots, 67

Caramel Popcorn, 78

CREAM CHEESE
Cream Cheese Baked Potato , 42
Cream Cheese Spinach, 44
Cream Cheese Cauliflower, 51
Cream Cheesecake Soufflé, 72
NY Cream Cheesecake, 82

EGGPLANT
Eggplant Ratatouille, 41
Marinated Eggplants with Sesame Seeds, 45
Eggplant & Zucchini Mix, 49
Tahini Eggplants , 51
Cilantro Eggplant Chips, 65

EGGS
Cheddar Eggs Burrito, 7
English Eggs Bacon Breakfast, 8
Baked Cheddar Eggs, 10
Egg Ham Rolls, 11
Running Cheddar Eggs, 16
Wrapped Bacon Eggs, 17
Egg Sandwich, 19
Eggs in Bacon Cups, 19
Avocado Eggs, 20
Bacon Eggs, 63
Parmesan Egg Clouds, 67
Milky Egg Custard, 69
Pumpkin Egg Mousse, 84

FENNEL
Thyme Fennel, 52

FETA
Feta Beet Cubes, 48
Feta Cheese Potato Slices, 52

FLOUR
Banana Pancakes, 18
Cream Cheesecake Soufflé, 72
Cake with Vanilla Frosting, 75
Banana Cinnamon Cake, 78
Chocolate Sugary Cupcakes, 79
Marble Cocoa Cake, 79
Milky Semolina Cake, 83

GARLIC
Garlic Catfish, 24
Garlic Ground Chicken, 26
Garlic Pork Satay, 34
Oregano Garlic Heads, 48
Salty Garlic Pretzels, 60

GOAT CHEESE
Figs with Goat Cheese, 63

HAM
Egg Ham Rolls, 11

KALE
Kale Chips, 62

LAMB
Thyme Lamb Ribs, 28
Cayenne Lamb Steak, 35
Rosemary Lamb Shank, 36

LEEK
Leek Parmesan Tarts, 20
Creamy Leek, 44

LEMON
Salty Lemon Artichokes, 39

LENTILS
Carrot Lentil Burgers, 40

MACARONI
Cheddar Mac'n'Cheese, 45

MILK
Milky Vanilla Toasts, 9
Milky Cod, 16
Milky Egg Custard, 69
Milky Semolina Cake, 83

MOZZARELLA
Mozzarella Sausage Stromboli, 13
Mozzarella Pepperoni Patties, 15
Mozzarella Radish Salad, 41
Bacon Mozzarella, 68

MUSHROOMS
Chicken Mushroom Rolls, 16

Cremini Mushroom Satay, 41
Cheddar Porto Mushrooms, 42
Mushrooms & Cream, 50
Cottage Cheese Mushrooms, 53

OATS
Oats Carrot Cookies, 6
Bacon Zucchini Boats, 10
Sugary Oatmeal Muffins, 12
Strawberry Oatmeal, 14
Cheese Oatmeal Fritters, 18
Chicken Oatmeal Schnitzel, 25
Oat Chicken Sausages, 37
Figs with Goat Cheese, 63
Banana Oatmeal Bites, 70
Oats Cookies, 72
Vanilla Oat Rolls, 77
Oat Chocolate Chip Cookies, 81

OKRA
Olive Oil Okra, 50
Corn Okra Bites, 57

ONION
Onion Chicken Skin, 32
Onion Green Beans, 40
Sweet Onion Rings, 50
Chili Onion Rings, 58

ORANGE
Orange Beef Mignon, 24

PAPRIKA
Cheddar Baked Paprika Toasts, 11
Paprika Soufflé, 15
Paprika Chicken Buns, 21
Paprika Corn Beef, 30
Ginger Paprika Shrimps, 35
Paprika Hasselback Potatoes, 45
Paprika Yellow Squash, 53
Pickles in Paprika, 62
Paprika Chicken Bites, 64

PARMESAN
Broccoli Parmesan Casserole, 6
Breakfast Parma Sandwich, 10
Parmesan Spinach Quiche, 19
Leek Parmesan Tarts, 20

Parmesan Chorizo Rolls, 21
Parmesan Peppers, 31
Parmesan Sweet Potato Casserole, 38
Asparagus & Parmesan, 39
Mexican Parmesan Corn, 51
Parmesan Zucchini Chips, 63
Parmesan Chicken Sticks, 66
Parmesan Egg Clouds, 67

PINEAPPLE
Pineapple Chicken Breast, 22

PORK
Pork Strips, 22
Salty Pork Belly, 25
Pork Chops, 26
Pork Bak, 31
Chili Pork Slices, 32
Oregano Pork Loaf, 33
Honey Pork Meatballs, 34
Garlic Pork Satay, 34
Pork Ribs, 37
Celery Pork Balls, 64
Sesame Pork Cubes, 67

POTATO
Turmeric Potato Pancakes, 7
Turmeric Potato, 9
Buttery Potato Scramble, 11
Tofu Potato Scramble, 12
Cheddar Potato Halves, 17
Cheddar Potato Gratin, 39
Cream Cheese Baked Potato , 42
Paprika Hasselback Potatoes, 45
Dill Mashed Potato, 46
Cream Potato, 47
Feta Cheese Potato Slices, 52
Creamy Red Potatoes, 54
Salty Potato Chips, 57
Carrot & Potato Balls, 66

PUMPKIN
Honey Pumpkin Mash, 18
Sugary Pumpkin Wedges, 43
Sweet Pumpkin Loaf, 69
Honey Pumpkin Delights, 71
Pumpkin Egg Mousse, 84

RAISINS
Raisins Carrot Pie, 69
Raisin Vanilla Muffins, 74

SALMON
Smoked Salmon Omelet, 20
Rosemary Salmon Steak, 29
Creamy Salmon Pieces, 68

SAUSAGE
Chicken Sausages, 6
Mozzarella Sausage Stromboli, 13
Oat Chicken Sausages, 37

SHRIMP
Ginger Paprika Shrimps, 35
Coriander Shrimp Cakes, 62

SPINACH
Parmesan Spinach Quiche, 19
Cream Cheese Spinach, 44
Spinach Fritters, 64

SQUASH
Butternut Squash Puree, 46
Chili Squash Wedges, 52
Paprika Yellow Squash, 53

STRAWBERRY
Strawberry Oatmeal, 14
Strawberry Cobbler, 84

THYME
Thyme Lamb Ribs, 28
Thyme Fennel, 52
Thyme Salty Tomatoes, 55

TILAPIA
Creamy Coriander Tilapia, 23

TOFU
Tofu Potato Scramble, 12

TOMATO
Tomato Beef, 35
Tomato Nutmeg Zucchini, 47
Cabbage with Tomato, 47
Thyme Salty Tomatoes, 55

Pepper Green Tomatoes, 59

TURKEY
Turkey Bread Reuben, 8
Maple Turkey Breast, 29
Dijon Turkey Legs, 30

WALNUTS
Toasted Salty Walnuts, 60
Walnut Baked Apples, 75

ZUCCHINI
Bacon Zucchini Boats, 10
Cheddar Zucchini Frittata, 15
Beef Zucchini Rings, 30
Spicy Zucchini Slices, 38
Tomato Nutmeg Zucchini, 47
Eggplant & Zucchini Mix, 49
Parmesan Zucchini Chips, 63

Manufactured by Amazon.ca
Bolton, ON

15103745R00050